1989

BEYOND Birth Control

✍ BEYOND Birth Control
The Christian Experience of Sex

SIDNEY CORNELIA CALLAHAN

SHEED AND WARD: NEW YORK

For my husband, Daniel,
and our children,
Mark, Stephen, John, Peter, Sarah, and David

Contents

Introduction

I WRITE this book about the relationship of sexuality and Christianity because of dissatisfaction with previous writing on the subject. Too often Christians retreat before the complex cultural changes that have been labeled "the sexual revolution." True, the Church crises over birth control and celibacy arouse concerned thinking—and there are perennial probings into problems of sexual morality. But, unfortunately, the piecemeal efforts to deal with each disturbing facet of changing sexual behavior only create more confusion. Tinkering with the rules and patching up doctrines does not work; a radical reappraisal and a new synthesis are needed.

I title this book *Beyond Birth Control* in order to empha-

size that the arguments over the acceptance or nonacceptance
of contraception are only a beginning. This generation needs
a whole new "philosophy" or "theology" or "structured approach" to human sexuality. Old answers and approaches
which were developed in other eras and within other sys-
tems of thought cannot be forced onto a community sensitive
not only to new insights in theology but to new social and
psychological complexities. In a new Christian approach to
human sexuality, what will be important?

As a first assumption, I see the resurrection of Christ and
ourselves as central. Christ's resurrection affirms God's power
and his love of man and creation. Christ lives with the God
of the living as a human being, and we too can live in the
fullness of time when "everything is present." So too, whatever the process of change in bodies, we continue as ourselves
in the new creation. As Brian Wicker says, "It is as necessary
for an encounter with Christ to be a bodily encounter as it
is for any other human encounter ... (There is no such thing
as a purely spiritual encounter.)"[1] Perhaps the stages of em-
bryonic life, birth, and growth demonstrate how individual
identity persists as a pattern within change. But the crucial
question in a Christian view of sexuality is whether sexual
identity and sense data continue in the new creation.

In the old rational, static view of eternity in which Christ's
resurrected humanness was ignored, complete disembodi-
ment seemed the ruling image of existence. At the most, a
glorified body was allowed only the distance receptors of sight
and hearing. However, the Eucharist and Christ's resurrec-

tion appearances also stress the senses of touch and taste; the whole man comes from God, and can live in God as a man among men. Surely, the Jews could not imagine such a divided view of man as "the ghost in the machine" or a salvation which was individual rather than communal. As we Christians recover our appreciation of the whole man living in a social community of man, we can see no reason to exclude sexuality from the communal human presence in the new creation. The human-to-human love and communication is not necessarily smothered and overwhelmed by the individual God-to-man relationship. John tells us that God loved us so we could love one another; this can hardly be limited to this life only. A great joy of heaven will be in the full love of each other. My question to the Christian tradition is this: Why should the greatest ecstasy and fullest expression in human-to-human loving be excluded in the "marriage of the Lamb"? The rigid distinctions traditionally made between the different kinds of love seem more verbal than real, or at worst a way "to purify" love from sexuality. Charity, friendship, parental love, and passion differ more in degree of reciprocal expression than in motivation.

I wish to argue that the only drawback with sexual ecstasy has nothing to do with the qualities so traditionally despised. Sexual eroticism, passion, spontaneity, present intensity, and ecstatic self-consciousness can be seen as valuable and important capacities of humanity. The only drawback now attributed to genital orgasm is its limited duration due to our time-space limits and its limiting exclusiveness based on the sexual identities and physical structuring of an adult male and female. A truly heavenly ideal could have the sexual one-flesh ecstatic union of the couple extended to all human relationships; all would be married to all, as the small child and mystic intuit. In loving, the first wound is not being able to marry one's parents and siblings and the last wound is not be able to marry everyone.

I also wish to show that the newest understanding of person and of sexual identity deplores the rigid cultural suppression which isolates and divides the sexes by imposing separate and different male and female identities. Sexual polarity and the couple mystique have stunted human personality development and harmed human community. A better concept of a human being can include growing into the fullness of human personality without self-limitations arising in an insecure clutching at male or female identity. As man reclaims his body-self and his social and communal nature, he regains erotic perception and communication between all persons while de-emphasizing the exclusive genital relationship of the exclusive couple. Play, tenderness, and aesthetic freedom complete the ecstatic compulsion of passionate genitality. When heterosexual polarity and sexual mystiques concerning male and female identity are de-emphasized, sexuality becomes more personal, more human, and more pleasurable.

However, it is also important that an ideal of resurrected sexuality include passion, and, if anything, be beyond genitality rather than regress to a pregenital childhood state. The prophets of a "polymorphously perverse" resurrected body, with every sense given equal value, deny the ego and the rational organization of personality which accompanies genitality's hierarchical development. When man's rationality, individuality, and the active adaption to reality is considered harmful and illusory, Christianity and the ideal of man lose their unique western disposition to passionate goal-directed activity in a good creation. The importance of future-directed goals of work and uses of intellect correspond to the importance granted genitality. Christian celibacy, therefore, should be motivated differently from the celibacy of an ego-denying, world-denying view of genital sexuality as contamination through involvement with the fleeting processes of the bonds of flesh. Christian celibacy can only be a choice made positively "for the sake of the kingdom," and a free choice made only by those "who can take it." It seems clear that this celibate state is not the negative choice of those who could not or would not marry, but a positive alternative for those fully capable of marriage.

In the chapter on celibacy, I wish to stress that the choice of Christian celibacy is a sacrifice for the sake of the community. One is not free *from* love and family, but free *for* more loves and a wider family. Giving up the joyful reciprocal relationship of a mate, the celibate makes all men his family, extending kinship and marital commitment to all, particularly those incapable of reciprocity or of sustaining their own families. The celibate person witnesses to the kingdom in living other forms of community and in his freedom to lay down his life for his friends. Celibacy mystiques involving virginal marriage to God or an ideal of unspotted exclusiveness of an undivided love of God owe more to paganism than to Christianity. As Rahner says, "God is no 'object' next to others. Man's intentionality cannot be directed to him as it is to the multiplicity of categorical objects and persons it meets."[2] Nor is celibacy more surely a better preparation for the resurrection than marriage once it is argued that the absence of marriage among the "sons of the resurrection" may not mean absence of sexual communication. Without our limitations of space and time, the complete giving of one to one and one to many might not be incompatible. Now celibates must sacrifice and sublimate to be "married to all," and only those graced with a naturally strong love of their own flesh and that of others can live without sexual confirmation. However, when "every tear is wiped away" and God is "all in all," then man's self-limitations for the sake of others will not be necessary. Celibacy and marriage may be both but preparations for a fuller freer communion.

However, since the kingdom has not yet come, sexual inhibition and sacrifical work remain a part of growing and loving. The resurrection perceived in our field of vision is a process of harvest. The first fruits of Christ's resurrection will gradually empower our own resurrection as we continue to work out our salvation with fear and trembling. There have always been those who, believing the kingdom completely come and themselves perfect and incapable of sinning, denied the need for any self-limitation. Many sects and secular movements espousing man's innate goodness have said that man needs only freedom and the lack of frustration and repression to develop. In the chapter on sexual development, I wish to stress that modern psychological insights speak of the individual's need of frustration and limits in order to become aware of outer reality and other people. Whether one discusses "sublimation," and "graduation," or our "griefs and discontents, the forces of change," the role of frustration and loss in human development becomes clear. The limits of reality spur us to grow and overcome. To grow and live in human community, individuals must die like the seed, give without measure, bear one another's burdens, and take up crosses. Inhibition and limiting morality, including a limiting of sexual morality, is inescapable for individual and communal development. A Christian morality of love seeks to reduce the burden to a minimum, to infuse the law with love and to temper it with mercy. To the new men the law remains only a supplemental and initial means to advance to freedom. Once sexuality is demythologized and humanized, sexual morality and sexual transgressions can take their proper place. Human sexuality, one of the very important human ways of self-expression and communication, can also be regressive or exploitative, but sexual failings are no worse or better than other human failings.

Those Christians attempting to redress past degradation of sexuality err when they assert that sexuality is "the essential way" by which human beings arrive at spiritual awareness.

The "inexhaustible mystery" of sexuality is not found in the erotic aspect or the physically ecstatic, but only in the relational dimension of sexuality. Somehow the mystery cult of sacred sex can never be at ease with irrational sexual pleasure here and now with real people. Only when the New Testament view of a demythologized sexuality which is simply *one* of man's important faculties is fully accepted can Christians freely accept sensual sexual pleasure, much less imagine full sexual completion beyond time in communal bodily resurrection. Once the static, over-rational, disembodied-spirit ideal gives way to an ideal of body-persons, dynamic movement, and the communal resurrection, then the Beatific Vision can also include images of the great city, the heavenly banquet, the drinking of living water, the marriage of the Lamb. The kingdom can be seen as including active play, validating pleasure for pleasure's sake.

Such a Christian reappraisal and new appropriation of sexuality brings with it a wider reappraisal of other appropriations in human life. In the chapter on procreation and control, we can see that the questions of human sexuality lead to the world, the human community, and the future of man. The question of population increase, added to the fact that the human community is on the threshold of biological and genetic control of human life, presents a crisis and challenge exceeding the crisis of harnessing atomic energy. One can visualize the human condition at present as a race within humanity between knowledge as power and knowledge as wisdom and insight. Only human wisdom can control the destructive potential inherent in power and use it for human goods. A new synthesis of psychological and social sciences with theology is needed now that we realize how much the inner man is shaped by forces beyond reason. To understand the unconscious, to understand social conditioning, casts light upon what reason can and cannot do and leads to a new dimension of decision-making.

In considering control and morality, the Church has gone wrong (in its sexual teaching and practice particularly) because it has either not known the force of the hidden factors shaping man, or when it has acknowledged the irrational, has been oversuspicious and despised it, opting for a completely rational ideal. Emotion and reason have been as severely severed as were the old concepts of body and mind. Science and human experience, however, have shown us the importance of evolutionary development, the importance of affect in man, and of the subtle dynamic interactions within man. To be free to live as ourselves and master our destiny (individual and collective), man must value and shape the irrational, giving it as much direction as he can. In the human species self-consciousness is basic and primary. "But," says Jean Rimaud, "this firm consciousness should be as completely as possible an integration of our entire ego, raising from the shadows into the light all that we can gather, either to accept it as it is, to take some of it and leave the rest, or to capture its impulses, utilizing their strength or orientating them at will, transmuting them, sublimating them."[3] The self can and must actively choose within the conditions in which it finds itself. The whole growth of ego psychology has reemphasized the traditional moral necessity of actively choosing behavior and striving to direct consciousness. But now, too, the validity and importance of emotion in itself is recognized; the accepting of feeling as it is, without sublimation, is important. It is also joyously human to actively accept and cooperate with forces beyond human mastery. A lover can welcome eroticism and passion just as a mother in childbirth can consciously and exultingly welcome the expulsive waves arising from within.

A new appreciation of sexuality accepts both passive and active aspects of reality. Human sexuality includes the simple experiences of the pleasures of warmth, touch, play, naturally enjoyed, spontaneously lived. One aspect of sexuality is akin to basking in the sun, splashing in the sea." But, besides play, there is also passion in sexuality which involves tension, physical exertion, a violent involuntary reaction, and pleasure raised to ecstasy. The intensity of these sexual experiences of self-consciousness and union have shrouded them with mystery and fear; genital sexuality has seemed in many cultures so different from most human experience that it must be suspect or divine. Christians committed to the restoration of the creation appropriate both dimensions of sexuality while asserting that other life experiences also give intense pleasure, motivation, and commitment. Human experience is a continuum marked by intense active moments and more relaxed passive times, but the gulf is not between sexual versus nonsexual experience (or natural versus supernatural). Within a dynamic developing continuum of human experience with its movement, pleasure and growth, sexuality is affirmed and yet directed to the human community. Christians are then set the task of developing an affirmative sexual paideia in which individual growth, pleasure, and joy, even pleasure for pleasure's sake, are interrelated with the good and the pleasures of the human community.

A new understanding including psychological, social, and cultural interrelationships emerges. Reason must fully recognize the irrational subjective factors in life: origins, processes, conditioning, and group behavior are added to "objective" biological truth, observation, will, and reasoning. A horizontal communal subjective dimension of life completes a vertical, individualistic, logical orientation. Subjective emotions and subtle weighing of value and cultural expectation will complete discernment. In my discussions of sexual behavior, marriage, and contraception, I will suggest what might be called an "integrity calculus" which includes emotions and the communal good; one can no longer simply take scripture, natural law, or traditional moral theology as the only framework. I assume that an individual should grow toward an integrity and wholeness of the personality which unifies belief, actions, and symbols with a love of others in the human community. In this process, sexuality is not sacred or more mysterious than the rest of life. Ideal sexual behavior, like other human ways of growing and communicating, demands self-respect, respect for the "inalienable dignity" of others given them by God apart from the community's evaluation, and respect for the welfare of the human community.

Unfortunately, one major hindrance to wholeness has been

an antiflesh mentality which became merged with an anti-woman prejudice. In the past women could not take a full participating part either in sexuality, marriage, childbirth, or the church and culture. Woman's subordination and submissive place arose because, as an embodied projection of sexuality, she was considered mysteriously different and inferior. Only when sexuality is demythologized, accepted, and enjoyed can women and woman's sexual functions be calmly accepted. Conversely, only when woman is an equal person can sexual intercourse be mutually personal and important. Christians newly affirming the body-person unity, sexuality, emotions, community, and communication will also newly affirm the importance of conception, childbirth, and childhood. Fortunately, power to transcend natural processes, given to Christians in vocations of celibacy or in controlling fertility, accompanies a new appreciation of the earliest hidden processes of human development. A fuller, deeper understanding of the complexity of human development and human relations brings new appreciation of the heretofore excluded world of women and children. The life in the family becomes the human equivalent of the hidden but extensive part of the iceberg under water. Children, adults, and cultures are changed by intimate emotions and early expectations of what it means to be human. A new human appropriation of emotions and sexuality can be combined with the traditional values of reason and work when people actually live this new integrity. Our only hope as a human community is in persons who together live a fuller human ideal so that their freedom frees others. For generations, in most human cultures, mankind has been sexually enslaved in one way or another, never integrating individual and communal passion, pleasures, and procreation. Is it too much to hope that today a new era of sexual balance begins?

NOTES

[1] Brian Wicker, *Toward a Contemporary Christianity,* University of Notre Dame Press, Notre Dame, Ind., 1967, p. 252.

[2] Karl Rahner, S.J., "Unity of Love of God and Love of Neighbor" in *Theology Digest,* Summer 1967, Vol. 15, No. 2, pp. 87-93.

[3] Jean Rimaud, S.J., "Psychologists versus Morality," in *Cross Currents of Psychiatry and Catholic Morality,* ed. by William Birmingham and Joseph Cunneen, Meridian Books, Cleveland, 1966, p. 130.

I

Sexuality and the Resurrection

THE ACCEPTED stance for writing about sexuality is half apologetic, with many allusions to our culture's great need for creative thinking. The strategy seems to consist of heroic efforts to make sexuality seem so boringly technical, biologically and/or theologically, that only a sense of duty impels persistence. Then we no longer need feel guilty at our fascination with the subject, but why pretend? Is not such high seriousness and ponderous prose merely another way to anesthetize floating anxieties and satisfy our ever-prevalent prudery?

Emotional involvement with sexuality is a mark of the human condition. Each one of us lives a life in which our sexual identity and development intimately affects us indi-

vidually, affects others, and affects our culture. Reverbera-
tions of love, affection, hate, hostility, euphoria, anxiety,
depression—the whole range of human emotions is involved
with sex. To discuss sexuality and leave out the personal
emotional dimension is a distortion. A realistic appraisal of
sexuality must be founded on the rock of human reactions
and emotions as well as on isolated scientific inquiries.

After frankly admitting the importance of emotions and
the attraction of emotionally charged subject matter, one
can also admit the intellectual fascination and challenge of
sexuality defined in a broad rather than narrow way. What is
the source of all this human emotion and activity? What does
it mean? Is there any purpose inherent in the sexual drive
apart from the obvious survival of the species? Does God
care? Not many people dare to issue proclamations at this
point, but everyone from playboy philosopher to pope confronts the questions.

Past and current exaggerations and mystiques of sexuality
can be criticized confidently, but when the times comes for
sound syntheses of the best secular knowledge and new
theology, the tone must become more tentative. Too much
remains unknown to do anything but probe gingerly and
attempt to bring forth new insights. But even at this point
things do need to be said in order to demythologize sexuality
and yet keep it human. Not many viewpoints do this. At
least three exaggerated visions of sexuality are current which
have diverse origins, subtleties, and ramifications, but are all
equally far from a balanced human view.

First comes the vision of sexuality as the mainspring of the universe. For true believers of this cult the drive toward copulation and male-female unity is man's primary driving force. Nothing else can be as important or worthwhile as achieving sexual release and enjoyment. While all else in life may be an illusion, touch confirms a "sensible" existence. Thinking may get you nowhere, seeing is not believing; but the credo *tango ergo sum* never fails. Feeling is reality, and the best feelings are found in sexual orgasms with stimulating partners of the opposite sex. With orgasm, the world turns—and man reaches his ultimate destiny. In this near-mystery religion of sexuality, it follows that the polarity of the sexes generates the creativity in the world. Phallus and womb are everywhere, beneath every cultural or rational phenomenon. The initiated always can find thrust and receptivity, activity and passivity, male and female creatively copulating. They say: Why fight reality? The present moment and the present sensation of pleasure are what count. Sex is what makes the world go round.

A second and even more radical form of sexual mystique makes the present sensation and every sensation of the body so important that genital sexuality itself becomes suspect. This newly subtle vision glorifies the pregenital sexuality of mankind. The equal value of every sensual delight, so goes this theory, has been threatened by the overwhelming drive for genital pleasure; for a person to achieve genital pleasure, all of the other means to delight have had to be repressed. The organization and repression called for in this development are really a tyranny of the genital drive toward procreation; and repressive cultures, with their interest in social reality and the future, have imposed an exclusive sexuality— i.e., genital sexuality—on the growing child. Norman O. Brown, modern prophet of completely unrepressed sexuality, describes the blessed state of infantile sexuality as being "polymorphously perverse." Without repression, Brown maintains, man can become "polymorphously perverse," so that the last and most powerful tyranny of man can be overthrown and "the resurrection of the body achieved." The paradise of undifferentiated pleasure which everyone experiences in the euphoria of infancy can thus be regained; and such a communion of love's body can redeem mankind.[1]

Obviously, of the two versions of sexual salvation, pregenital versus genital, the pregenital paths to paradise have less general appeal than the ever-popular faith in genital experience. Unless the movement to mystic participation in reality through such means as drugs and oriental philosophies become a mass movement, genital sexuality and male-female mystiques will remain triumphant. Observers who proclaim that "sex is dead" are a bit premature. A more perceptive analysis of the situation might use Marshall McLuhan's criteria of "hot" and "cool" media, and say that sexuality has already cooled among the avant-garde today and may be cooling for the masses tomorrow. The "hot" media approach, on the other hand, with its concepts of ready-made content, definition, organization, and goal, would emphasize male-female polarity and the genital sex imperative to achieve orgasm. Pregenital sex would be more "cool" since it lacks focus, organization, and definition; with "cool" media, people have to actively supply meaning. However, taken in perspective, even a cooled-down sexual mystique presents a distorted view of reality. Whatever the temperature, the current preoccupation with sexuality is fevered and can only be understood as a violent reaction to another extreme: the third exaggerated vision of sexuality.

This third viewpoint is that ancient suspicion of sexuality which reigned as recently as the late-late Victorian era. This distortion proclaims the special evil of the sexual drive and arises from a disassociated view of the human being, "the ghost in the machine" approach. In this model of man, mind and body are distinct and opposite, indeed split and warring against one another. The "higher" rational being in man—variously labeled as mind, soul, spirit—pines imprisoned in the body. The spirit chafes at physical limitations and at the body's "lower" drives, which are most powerfully at work in sexuality. Man longs to be free and completely devoted to the higher human realities without the distractions and disorders of the flesh. The body can aspire to be but a good instrument, a worthy servant, a docile "brother ass."

The stoic answer to this disassociated view of man is rational control and unconditional surrender of the "lower" faculties to the "higher" mind and will. Man would be more pure and perfect if he never had to contaminate the eternal rational part of his being, but in the human condition dutiful use of the body can include a limited exercise of sexuality.

Since the survival of the species depends upon procreation and the family, sex must go on. An extreme manichaean view might deplore concessions to procreation, but the milder stoic forms see procreation as a duty to society which must be borne by the nonelect incapable of celibacy and complete self-control.

Such an exaggerated antisexual position is now very much out of fashion. Few would admit today to such hostile interpretations of "the flesh." A few fundamentalist sects and a few unregenerate theologians might go the whole way and throw in the dangers of the devil to boot, but most modern Christians find this heritage only embarrassing. Since these same Christians cannot deny that great Christian saints have held and taught distorted antisexual doctrines, many make amends by enlisting in the currently popular pro-sexual mystiques. Along with other rank-and-file cultists, however, they retain latent antisexual ways of thinking which crop up at crucial moments.

Unfortunately, current Christian views of sexuality often include the worst of both extreme pro-sexual mystiques and latent antisexuality. After breathless prose devoted to the awe, mystery, love, and I-Thou encounter of sexuality, a priest can calmly state: "Sexual experiences have, of themselves, something of a stupefying nature in the strong sense of the term."[2] Another even more insistent lay defender of "the utterly central position occupied by sex, its depth, and the mystery that invests it," can also worry about controlling the "passionate, fierce" tendencies of the body which can give way to the "oppressive intoxicating breath of fleshly lust."[3] Augustine's attitudes are lurking beneath the surface rhetoric. Disgust at becoming "all flesh" in intercourse echoes the stoic horror of being subject to irrational emotion. When another priest-theologian sympathetic to the goodness of sexuality can stress "ever-greater control" and "mystical prayer at the moment of climax,"[4] then the fundamental suspicions of emotion and the body's processes appear clearly. The "ghost in the machine" is still with us; even if sex is now a fine part of the machine, we are still using "it."

The underlying assumption that man is divided into separate compartments remains a formidable hurdle for any human attempting to live a fully integrated life. How is it possible to appropriate the new secular knowledge and theories of the undivided self? How can new theologies be developed to overcome the persistent views of man's inner divisions which so distort sexuality?

For a start, men can meditate on and review for themselves all the evidence for knowing the self to be a dynamic unity of body and mind. Both the testimony of man's intuition and his new scientific knowledge belie the static divided view of human reality. Physics, biology, and chemistry have shown that bodily existence is a fluctuating organic process in time. Human life consists of unbelievable activity and interaction of different processes from the moment of conception to death. The most complex interaction within the organism and with the external environment determines the course of all life. But the greatest potential to affect existence is that unique factor in the human species: self-consciousness. In man the brain becomes dominant, self- and social-consciousness develop, and experience can be symbolized in gesture, speech, art, and writing. Activity arising in the complicated human brain can create myriads of entities that exist independent of their origin. The human brain is still material, however; it can be controlled and affected by material means such as drugs, electrical charges, deprivation of food and sleep. New researches in conditioning behavior, psychosomatic medicine, and the mechanisms of sleep have explored the complex interactions of body, brain, and consciousness. We are our physical processes, while we are more; we are organisms and persons. We know we are not just prisoners inside a mechanism because the links between physical existence and personality are too intimate, too central to existence. Yet we are also more than a functioning organism, if for no reason other than that we remember our past and can project our identity and rational activity into the unknown future; we possess recall and foresight. With this peculiar human ability, man, being man, also continually searches for some meaning to these processes. Why am I conscious of myself being conscious of both my physical processes and my consciousness?

Self-conscious identity is a true wonder. How does a mature middle-aged man remain the same person he was as a small child, the same person he will be as an old, shriveled man? Even more awesome, how does a microscopic bundle of cells contain the potential for such processes of growth. Growth and change with identity retained is the disturbing miracle of concrete life. Accordingly, a certain group of rationalists have always shied away from confronting the turmoil and disorder of chance, growth, and coming-to-be. When Athena sprang full-grown from the brow of Zeus and never aged, her genesis and destiny conformed to one dream of reason. But this static timelessness remains but a deluded dream. Modern physics and biology proclaim the human body to reflect an enduring informational pattern, with its own laws of operation and development imposing temporary order upon a conglomerate of materials and forces. These organisms, in turn, are being affected by an array of forces and materials in the environment. All is flux except the patterns, but patterns are significant.

Our vocabularies contain words which specifically attempt to express our sense of self-continuity amidst flux, words like "self," "form," "mode," "way of being," "self-system," "configuration." Karl Rahner even speaks of a polyvalent "forma corporis" so that the soul realizes possibilities of its own; for him "the body" is "the symbolic reality of man."[5] But to use these philosophically loaded words and concepts without extended philosophical discussion and argument is unsporting. Minimally speaking, perhaps all who study man can agree that certain patterns of human development emerge which relate the individual identity and life-cycle to the life of communities. Furthermore, a tentative consensus can be found for the thesis that human biological development accompanies a development of the reasoning powers and a development of emotional capacities. Thus all could say that, usually at adolescence, a capacity for abstract logical thought emerges, just as genital desires develop and social integration into the adult work world becomes important to both the individual and group. As the physical organism reaches maturity, objectivity, other people, and expanded interests can better enter the subjective life experience of the individual self.

Since every human group values certain habits of behavior in their members, they transmit expectations to the human young at all stages of growth. Particular cultures develop their own consensus of "virtues" and ideal characteristics for group emulation and individual appropriation. Along with mental and physical development, character development is expected to appear. With great wisdom Erik Erikson posits his illuminating writings on the solid basis of a human life-cycle with interrelated stages of growth toward maturity and integrity.[6] In the Eriksonian synthesis, man needs values in order to survive; he must develop appropriate virtues at different levels of sexual and mental development. The family and society naturally play an enormous part in fostering individual development, in providing "environmental releasers." And, in turn, the family and society are affected by the results of human growth.

In such an overall view of the development of human beings and human communities, sexuality is obviously a very important factor. Sexual development overlaps and interacts with mental development, ego development, and the social and economic structures of a society. However, both sexual mystiques and antisexual suspicions have isolated and exaggerated the importance of sexuality in human life. A more adequate reading of reality sees sexuality as one of several very important developmental processes in human life. While human sexuality is one of the prime ways that the self knows itself, becomes itself, and reaches out to others, speech and thought and work are other important means of self-realization, of communication with the community and the world. As long as people keep exalting one important human capacity over all the others, mankind becomes involved in distortions and confusions. Verbalism, rationalism, work mystiques, sex cults—all are destructive to the integrity and unity of human life and culture. Human reality cannot be reduced solely to language, to thought, to labor or libido. At the beginning of human life, for instance, in the stage labeled "oral," a baby seeks self-preservation and satisfaction in sucking, but he also begins to communicate through pre-verbal noises, to sort out sense impressions, and to explore and master his muscles and the environment. Sexuality can be explored well only if the other important ways of self-knowledge and self-expression and communication are also kept in mind.

In our western culture, ignorance of human sexual development and revulsion at bodily processes have sorely damaged, limited, and distorted the human development of both individuals and communities. Only recently have most students of human development accepted the general outline of sexual development through the so-called "oral," "anal," and "phallic" stages of heterosexual genitality. Experts may argue over the specific details, but as Harry Stack Sullivan explains it, the places where inside tissues connect with less sensitive outside tissues (mouth, anus, genitals) are bound to be the focus of specially intense sensations.[7] When biological survival and interpersonal relationships are also focused on these sensitive areas of the body, then what goes on there contributes to individual learning and personality development. The way we love ourselves and others depends upon interpersonal relationships begun when the infantile and young human is growing and learning at a phenomenal rate of speed. Moreover, each of these stages of growth—or "graduations," as Erikson terms them—seems to include a giving up of a means of satisfaction in order to obtain a more complete as well as more complex satisfaction. Each new growth is built upon a previous synthesis. As all the progressive sexual and social steps are taken, the development of the individual is harmonized into a whole personality.

True maturity will eventually reach the stage Erikson calls "generativity," a willingness to procreate and take responsibility for the next generation, a willingness to sustain the family and larger community. The sexual mark of maturity is generally labeled "genitality." Erikson describes genitality with these words: "Genitality, then, consists in the unobstructed capacity to develop an orgastic potency so free of pregenital interferences that genital libido (not just the sex products discharged in Kinsey's 'outlets') is expressed in heterosexual mutality, with full sensitivity of both penis and vagina, and with a convulsion-like discharge of tension from the whole body." But then he adds wryly, "This is a rather concrete way of saying something about a process which we really do not understand."[8]

Efforts to understand genitality by recording, measuring, and tabulating have been made by a whole new field of sex researchers. These social scientists and medical or biological specialists employ the usual tools of modern technical investigation, and measurements and quantification naturally become all-important. Just as naturally, moralists and psychoanalysts are appalled at such a specialized approach to human beings; they express the opinion that Kinsey should never have left the study of wasps. And more furor has been raised by the studies presented in *Human Sexual Response* by Dr. William H. Masters and Virginia E. Johnson. Movies, recordings, and personal laboratory observation of male and female masturbation and couples in coitus have all been used to amass technical details of sexual response. Such techniques are scorned by many with the accusation that they cultivate the ability of both researcher and subject to disassociate and repress appropriate human emotions. Many argue that it is just such uses of technology that create the "lack of affect" which ruins sexuality as a human activity. As one psychoanalyst observed in a bitter comment on the inroads of technical thinking: "The quite preposterous situation arose in which the patient sought treatment for ejaculatio praecox or impotence, and the healer sought to find out whether he liked his partner."[9]

In technical approaches to sex, the liking and the loving

part of life are relegated as "psychic factors." Measurement and quantification can only apply to blood pressure, bodily secretions, muscular contractions, skin flush, and other physical details which do not add up to love. Even the individual body gets lost in the statistical measurements of its parts. The danger of technical approaches to sex, especially in marriage books, is the old problem of treating the body as a machine which, when properly worked, will produce certain results. By overstressing technique and achievement, man can get so disassociated from his body that impotence and frigidity become more frequent. As Paul Ricoeur says so well: "Sexuality remains basically foreign to the 'intention-tool-thing' relationship."[10] Even the current mystiques and old suspicions at least recognize that sex transcends tension outlets. Orgasms are more than vaso-congestion, myotonia with 5-12 contractions at 0.8-second intervals. With human beings, more interesting questions arise: Why do certain physical reactions bring pleasure? Why do men seek "tension outlets"? Why do these physical sensations feel good?

Those who argue that the brain is man's primary sexual organ have a point. The brain's interpretation of the physical sensation seems all-important. Contractions and spasms can bring great pleasure; they can also cause great pain. Sensitivity to touch can stimulate and intensify desire; it can also cause revulsion at physical contact. In disorders of sexuality, fear and anxiety inhibit the interpretation of sensation as pleasure. Such disorders raise complex questions, but why things go right is even more complex.

Pleasure, including sexual pleasure, may have something to do with a pleasure center in the brain. But even if research fully confirms it, are not efforts to pinpoint pleasure only equal to efforts to "place" the soul in the heart or the breast or the pineal gland? Of course, one aspect of pleasure is the stilling of a biological need, the release of tension, as in eating when hungry, drinking when thirsty, evacuating when full, etc. Normally, these releases from tension are biologically pleasurable in themselves. In man, however, is not the primary pleasure in the heightened self-consciousness that gives him a sense of identity in time? His senses are revealing to him that he is here and doing things; he experiences delight in the drama of existing in the moment.

But pleasure is also social, and relationships to others become intimately involved with the primary tension releases. We can almost totally agree with the profound observation that "all pleasure is societal—nature does not know real pleasure but only satisfaction of want."[11] In man satisfaction of want gives pleasure by increasing self-consciousness; when this is joined with communication and interaction with others, pleasure becomes far greater. One could argue that even primary self-consciousness is first given by others in society; but whichever comes first or is causal, a convergence and community of the self with others gives the greatest joy. Eating, talking, working, playing, and thinking together give man pleasure. Human beings delight in company, community, and communication. Since mature sexual pleasure arises from an intimate, completely absorbing form of communication between two people, it is not surprising that it has been heralded as the greatest of human delights. Thinking about pleasure gives us more understanding of sex than mystiques, suspicions, or scientific measurements.

There is the primitive joy in sex of being both intensely conscious of one's self through violent physical sensations and at the same time conscious of and close to another. Pleasure in physical closeness may derive from the euphoria of the babe in the womb or at the breast, or reflect the union of humanity in one species, or the mystical body, or all of these at once. Still the physical near-union produces a violent joy in the momentary near-conquest of man's spatial isolation and aloneness. In much the same way, a sexual consciousness of tense expectation with a final release in protean physical convulsion gives man a pleasurable confrontation with time. This is the joy of coming-into-being, captured in a particular moment of time: the curtain going up, the crescendo of trumpets, the chrysalis emerging, all forms of birth. Suspense, surprise, the explosion, the fall, the dive, the takeoff, the blooming— the experience of time gives man pleasure. Sensing the inevitability of orgasm in the moment before orgasm is a high point in this exquisite pleasure. It may be that this relationship to an experience of time is why delay and obstacles have been seen to increase pleasure. In all the traditions of romantic love, pleasure is intensified through anticipation and delay. The chase, denials, false starts, protestations—all prolong the excitement and serve to increase the emotional pleasure in time by prolonging love with obstacles.

Yet the experience of time and space can also bring anxiety

and sadness. When consciousness is so heightened, man realizes his limitations and brief existence in the world. An intense experience of time can also become a confrontation with death. Freud noted that something "in the nature of the sexual instinct is unfavorable to the achievement of absolute gratification,"[12] and that something may be the fact that ecstasy fades so quickly and physical unity is incomplete. The experience of self in limited time and space gives the pleasure, but it also frustrates the limitless desire. When union and passion have strained the boundaries of human life, death, the final swoon, may be seen as the only completion—the love-death pacts of passionate couples. Man is attracted to the involuntary, irrational forces of life which are also threats. Death may be seen as the final conquest of time and space, but it may also be seen as the final immersion in the overwhelming forces beyond man's limits. If great anxiety over death and self-annihilation prevails, then sexuality too will be seen as perilous.

Since death is the biological price of individuality (if it can't be killed, then it isn't alive and distinct), birth and life do foreshadow death in a sense. The intense manifestation of life in sexual experience *can* remind man of death, to the extent that intercourse has been called "a little death." In all probability man's repeated assertion that "all animals are sad after intercourse" stems from his own basic human anxiety about intense confrontations of time, space, and death. Whatever may be the case with animals, man is sad only if his particular culture conditions him to be anxious, the message being given by various forms of cultural prohibitions and taboos. If man has either a pagan or Christian assurance that the limitations of time, space, flesh, and death form a meaningful pattern, then a sense of relaxed well-being and joy can be the usual result of sexual experience. The sexual experience of release and renewal might also be labeled "a little birth." Mild euphoria after birth and lovemaking are as typical in man as mild anxiety, and far more appropriate.

Man's abilities of recall and foresight, as well as his sociability, allow him to expand sexual pleasure. One of the more subtle delights in mutual genitality is the consciousness of human participation in an overall pattern. Not only is there the satisfaction of the sensations and the pattern of the immediate experience, but the sense of being part of a much more complex, ongoing dance. An age-old primitive pleasure in repetition, procession, and ritual cycles is open to the individual loving couple who accept their humanity. Moreover, a long history to their unique relationship with its own projected future adds another dimension to the immediate pleasure. Awareness of past joys and of the unique progeny who have been born from their union gives an intuition of a continuing experience of birth and renewal incarnate in a mutual history. Even the past sufferings and struggles of an individual couple give the immediate pleasure resonance and a more intense quality. Memory and future expectations, cooperation and communication in other areas of their life—a whole range of complex human relationships influence the couple's pleasure in their sexual relationship.

Pleasurable physical reaction can expand or contract according to the personal emotional intensity inherent in the interpersonal communication. In an illicit affair, the social obstacles and residual fear and guilt can provide the person-to-person intensity that a fully shared family life and long fidelity give. While motives of abandonment and sacrilege may intensify pleasure in generally prudish cultures, personal motives and values can also add delight and joy. Even general religious affirmations may have some effect, if one can believe those surveys showing religious women more open to complete physical release (their confident acceptance of patterns? or of the irrational?). It is a myth to think that either illicit or virtuous love is automatically more pleasurable. It all depends on culture and circumstance.

In any case, much depends upon the persons involved trusting more to play, desire, love, and the irrational than to technique, analysis, and willpower. Too much self-consciousness, too much analysis—or striving of the will, can destroy the relaxation and playful quality necessary to evoke a response that partly wells up from the unconscious. Sexual pleasure is more of a gift than an achievement. All pleasure, and particularly the pleasure of sexuality, is bound up with the spontaneous urge to play. Play is free activity, a delight in exploring human potential and possibilities for themselves alone, without the bind of necessity. Desire rather than reasoned duty motivates free activity.

The capacity of human beings to be active for pleasure alone is a measure of their freedom. A whole history of cul-

ture can be written of man as the playing animal par excellence. Play is intimately related to culture, contemplation,
and through sexuality to human wholeness and healthy
equilibrium. With sexual play, pleasure must be the mainspring of activity; pleasure is a means of recovering and en-
joying the unconscious dimensions of man which are not
tapped in rational, purposive activity like work or abstract
thought. Man at play can be a man momentarily freed from
achievement goals.

Sexual pleasure, then, seems to have two levels. Man is de-
lighted by the irrational violent process, the very involuntari-
ness of release which renews the self through escape from
control and isolation. But man also finds joy in a very relaxed,
free-playing sexuality, a self-giving apart from the urgency of
desire. Whether these are pregenital or genital pleasures,
"hot" or "cool," they must be gotten together and integrated
in fully complete relationship. So too, the nonsexual context
shapes both levels of pleasure, which expand or contract with
different times, moods, and circumstances. Those who have
tried to explain away sexual pleasure by considering it nature's bribe for reproduction miss the point that reproduction
itself is also pleasurable. All of these processes could have been
as automatic as breathing or as instinctual as the reproduction
of ants. If sexual pleasure is but a bribe to man from nature,
man could have been bought at a far less handsome price, as
the addiction to alcohol, cigarettes, or drugs proves so de-
pressingly. The exuberant gratuity of irrational sexual pleasure is as inexplicable as man's response to beauty.

The experience of pleasure, whether it be in sexual activity or in speech, work, or thought, brings up some ultimate questions about man and the world. Traditional Christian doctrines of God and creation envision a reality in which all pleasure has basis and meaning. Human pleasure in self-consciousness, in activity and communion with others, is a reflection of God's nature. Although God can rejoice freely in himself, he chooses gratuitous creation and community with man. Since God made man in his own image, one mark of man's special place in the universe is his self-consciousness and ability to pleasure in himself, the world, and others. Of course, man's ability to think, speak, and work purposefully also reflects God's image, but Christian tradition has always insisted that man's free, gratuitous ability to love and play reflects a God of love who freely created man to love and enjoy him forever as well as to know and serve him forever. Creation is the work of God, but it is also God's play. Joy is integral to the universe.

Part of this joy is the joy of human relationships which can be focused and expressed in the sexual relationship of man and woman. The fruitful two-in-oneness of the Genesis couple was a gift from God; human procreation and joy in unity were given by God the Creator who saw that what he had made was good. In any new Christian synthesis attempted today, the Genesis affirmation of the couple's love, unity, and procreation will include an affirmation of the pleasure and joy in this gift. The fall of man and the disorder of the world have naturally affected man's sexuality and sexual relationships (as all other relationships), but sexual drive and sexual pleasure are still from God and have the same creative potential as all of man's capacities. Man's sexuality remains good though wounded. Never need we be as pessimistic as a modern follower of the Reformers who says "that the deeper we penetrate into or experience creation, the more manifest becomes the rift in creation."[13]

Those who see such a rift also see as central to this rift a deep division between man's sexual love and God's love, between "eros" and "agape." But why should a great gulf and difference in quality distinguish the loves that God gives humanity? Man's love for mother, sibling, friend, mate, children, country, and God is essentially the same. A self seeks a reciprocal relationship with another in which the giving and getting gives pleasure and joy. There may be different degrees of giving and getting in the various relationships of love, and there certainly are different degrees of physical expression. But, essentially, even such seemingly opposite loves as charity for an enemy and sexual desire for a beloved are alike. In both relationships I desire the well-being (literally) of another person and I desire to obtain and be in community with that person, although my expression of community will be very different. Friendship, coming somewhere between these two extremes of expressiveness, would share in the physical reserve of the one and the intimacy of the other.

Human love, like God's love, is freely given to each man in infancy; it is not dependent upon the worthiness of the person loved or upon his response. God is incredibly better at loving than we are, but there exists no incomprehensible gulf between divine and human love. The continuity between every level of human love is intuited by poet, mystic, and psychoanalyst, while scripture is filled with human analogies to describe God's love. Has it not been unfounded suspicion of the physical violence of sexuality and unwarranted fear of the self's assertion that have imposed rigid classifications and false separations on man's loving. Once the platonic body-soul schism is overcome, man's "higher" and "lower" loves no longer remain. All love seeks embodiment, expresssion, and reciprocal communal experience.

Traditional Christianity affirms that the incarnation was motivated by God's love and desire to become one with his people. And no "higher" or "spiritual" reserve kept Christ from the emotional physical self-giving (and self-assertion and self-completion), to and for man, in the act aptly called his passion. Christ's behavior, in which he showed forth the Father, could never be shaped to the stoic ideal of nonemotional rationalism.

Throughout his ministry, Christ gives the impression of complete human integrity, of an undivided human self. He is always himself. He lives fully the human processes of his life. He eats and drinks; he shares with others food and wine. He cures, through faith, but using spittle, mud, and touch. He weeps over the death of a friend and washes the feet of his disciples. He embraces the children, embraces John, and praises the fallen woman who in love and repentance washes his feet with her tears and dries them with her hair. There is no shrinking from women (clean or unclean), no worry over unseemly emotion or ritual pollution. Sexuality seems accepted as an integral part of life, as open both to sinful distortion and to blessed life in the kingdom. In Christ's teaching, as much if not more attention is given to man's work, words, and property as to his sexual behavior. In practice, mercy is bestowed equally upon unjust tax collector and adulteress. At the same time, high ideals for integrating the inner and outer man emerge in the preaching of love of God and one's neighbor. Inner love must be shown in concrete actions of healing, feeding, anointing, and obeying commandments. While claiming that fasting, prayer, faith, and his own power are at work in his acts of healing, Christ displays both great emotion and physical effort. For the great healing of mankind, he predicts, he must suffer and die for others as the ultimate expression of an inner, giving love. His dying is completely concrete and totally human.

Wondering at the example of Christ's undivided life and death, Christ's resurrection becomes crucial. In a Christian probing of sexuality, any questioning of the value and importance of our so-called "bodily processes" becomes incomplete without a discussion of the effect of the resurrection upon ourselves as human beings.

Some Christians today hold that the resurrection was something that happened to the disciples rather than to Jesus, that the disciples' increase in love led them into experiences which they inaccurately expressed as encounters with a resurrected body continuous with the Jesus they had known before death. According to this thesis, the discovery of Jesus' bones rotting in the hills of Judea would not be disturbing, since those dry bones could have no connection, or should have no connection, with Christ's life in God. This argument maintains that all the traditional testimony to Christ's resurrected body can be explained by wishful hallucination, deluded interpretation of subjective experience, or deliberate use of objective literary forms to express subjective truths. Paul, too, was misinformed and/or misinterpreting his own Damascus experience. When Paul says, "And if Christ has not been raised then our preaching is useless and your believing it is useless; indeed, we are shown up as witnesses who have committed perjury before God,"[14] he speaks for his own time and place only. In our present time of Christian maturity, man can recognize the closed causal continuum of history and can demythologize and purify the Christian faith.

The inevitable conclusion of this line of thought is clear. The body of the man Jesus Christ who lived in Palestine did not and does not live on in any form, and neither will we. If there is a future, or another world of God somehow, we do not participate in a way continuous with our present embodied selves. The new life or order or kingdom will be a complete break from this creation. Matter as we know it in consistent patterns, with sense perceptions and our individual life histories as embodied selves relating to other embodied selves, has no continuity or ultimate validity. If no body has ever had its self-identity (based upon a continuous pattern in time) survive the disintegration and dissolution of the death process which ends its identity in time, then man's view of himself is much affected. He becomes again a temporary conglomerate of elements with but a future destiny of fertilizing the soil in which his body will rot.

Furthermore, if no individual identity pattern has or could ever have broken through human death processes, how can any idea or experience or revelation have entered the human processes which were not already inherently there? Man, the evolved Interpreter of his experience and world, stands alone in the universe; he is his own judge and the only agent of any human salvation. The temporary purposeless quality of each individual body-self means that all its continuity and value must be given by the group which alone will survive and which alone has the right to enforce sanctions and determine morality, including sexual morality. The value of bodies and the right and wrong of sexual practices will be determined by the group interpretation rather than by response to any revealed purpose and will for human body-selves.

If this drastic argument against the resurrection of Christ be true, then the reinterpratation of Christianity must be total. Nor could Orthodox Judaism and the validity of the Old Testament stand within a closed causal continuum which so invalidates the New Testament and the traditional interpretations of Christians through history. If no messages have come from God except those man manufactures, then creation, death, pleasure, and human individuality remain completely mysterious and meaningless. Man is so completely one with himself as body that with no resurrection of the body only oblivion lies in the future. There is then no significance to human growth, to individual development. As the young German theologian Pannenberg warns: "When we discuss the truth of the apocalyptic expectation of a future judgment and the resurrection of the dead, we are dealing directly with the foundation of the Christian faith."[15]

Set over against a stoic confrontation of individual extinction is the Good News of the gospel. The resurrection affirms the continuous identity of the man Jesus before death and after glorification. The "oblivion" of death ends . . . and the theological dispute over God's reanimation of Christ's body begins. Typically, a Dutch theologian claims simple reanimation has never been claimed, while an English theologian claims that reanimation has never been denied by Orthodox Christians.[16] Yet, surely, Orthodox Christianity maintains that in the resurrection Christ "testified in word and deed to his bodily existence."[17] Admittedly, it is only with difficulty that confirmation of the empty tomb and reanimation can be separated from the central assertion of self-identity in resurrection. But, even in nature, the seed for a new plant sometimes withers or all but the husk is absorbed in the new organism. The placenta is discarded after human birth with no harm done to the newborn body. Moreover, St. Paul speaks of being instantly changed, of the resurrected body as a "spiritual body." The fact that Mary and the disciples did not immediately recognize Jesus might also be used to show the "newness" of the risen body and its commensurate new powers over old dimensions of space, time, and matter.

The reality of the empty tomb and reanimation, however,

is not consistent with other Christian experience. Scripture's testimony is rather detailed and complex to be but a symbolic message. The transfiguration and the mastery of nature implied in the walking on water and other miracles, especially the reversal of corruption in the raising of Lazarus, implies that the body's continuity from conception to resurrection can be unbroken. The Old Testament witness to certain prophets being assumed, along with the tradition of Mary's assumption, might also be relevant when correlated to Christ's words about his intimacy with Old Testament figures and his testimony to resurrection: "God is a God of the living." The seed may not wither away; after it bursts open (birth-death), it may be incorporated into the new organism and new life. After all, the embryo and the man are one, though this identity is not immediately apparent; growth, the demarcation point of birth, and then more growth transform and transfigure the identical human body. Through the death and resurrection of Christ the Firstborn, the great birthing begins.

The human continuity implied in the transcendence of the resurrection affirms the goodness of the first creation. Our individual bodily existences are validated by the resurrection of Christ's body: "The body is for the Lord." In a triumph of love for the world, God-become-flesh incorporates man into his own life. The event transcends history and fulfills and transfigures the laws of the first creation, but it does not destroy them. The glorified risen Christ ate with his disciples, walked and talked with them, and offered to let Thomas touch his wounds. Luke reports Christ's efforts to convince his disciples of his identity: " 'It is I indeed. Touch me and see for yourselves; a ghost has no flesh and bones as you can see I have' . . . 'Have you anything here to eat?' And they offered him a piece of grilled fish, which he took and ate before their eyes."[18]

Karl Rahner has said that the question of what happened when the risen Christ ate has never been theologically explored. It shoud be, for the mystery of a resurrected, glorified body eating everyday food may be a parable of incarnation and resurrection. Time, space, death—all the limiting categories of life have been transcended without losing the concrete individuation of humanity. The natural and the supernatural have become one reality. The risen Lord prepares and eats fish with his disciples; a first meal in the new creation is eaten by tired, sweaty fishermen pervaded by the smell of fish. The completely familiar and known coexists with incredible mystery and joy. In the resurrection a totally new dimension of life and joy completes and fulfills the past promises, pleasures, and desires of creation and humanity.

But what of human sexuality in the resurrection and new creation? Does this important way of self-appropriation and communication with others continue in those who rise and live in Christ? Many answers have been given in Christian history, and they have all reflected and affected Christian attitudes toward sexuality. During times of extreme anti-sexual prejudice, when the body and sexuality were thought to be particularly bound up with sin, the resurrected were

envisioned as neuter wraiths, as little more than eyes with
which to enjoy a beatific vision and perhaps ears to hear the
music of the spheres. When the Pauline "flesh" that wars
against the spirit was equated with the body and its processes, then the more suppression of these processes in this life
and the next, the more spiritual the existence. The mortification of a Simeon Stylites standing immobile upon his pillar
staring at the sun was an apt preparation for such a resurrection.

In the antisexual stance of most of Christian history (when,
as Rahner has noted, in the west there was a shrinking of a
theology of the resurrection before juridical approaches to
Good Friday), angelic theories of sexuality held sway.
Christians tried in their daily life to have mind, rationality,
and spirit suppress and annihilate physical processes so that,
like the angels, they could live as pure spirits. Naturally, this
purely spiritual, disembodied life was seen as the goal of resurrection—complete, though less naturally, with all the
nonspirit symbols of wings, lighted halos, and shining trans-
parencies. If the blessed were not quite bound to be pure
neuter spirits, they would be as perfectly celibate as the elite
had striven to be in an "angelic" life on earth. Of all the
"disreputable" physical aspects of the body which would
wither, sexuality would wither most completely. Christians
were to prepare for the resurrection by cultivating the higher
spirit and suppressing the lower flesh. Mortification of the
body and celibacy were basic requirements for serious Christians.

But what of our own day, when all this has changed, when Christianity affirms the body and turns again to a theology of the whole man? What of human sexuality and the resurrection? What is the ultimate purpose and meaning of sexual identity and interaction with others? This, of course, confronts us immediately with the question of Christ's celibacy and the recommendation of this way for the sake of the kingdom. The subject of celibacy demands a chapter of its own, but the question remains whether human sexuality is preparing man for an eternal fullness of life—and, if so, how?

The married incorporate their sexual expression in an intimate love-work relationship. Through the privilege and joy of sexual love and procreation, the married gain insight into God's creative impulse of love. In loving one person and one's children, a human being can better understand God's love and care for all. Promise, commitment, concern, spring from love. But there is also a foretaste of bliss in the gift of sexual pleasure. The delights and joys of sexual orgasms may be a preparation for heaven. Fallen man needs a training in joy, among other things. Sexual ecstasy can confirm the message of the beauty of the world. There is a gratuitousness in the universe and man; man is often "surprised by joy"—and much of this joy comes from sexuality.

Moreover, it is just the "suspicious" elements of sexuality which may be most important in preparing man for a new intensity of life. Violent desire and violent release serve to break through the sluggish inertia of man. In sexual experi-

ence man knows what it is to want something and what it is
to get it. In moments of intense sexual desire there arises a
collected concentration of attention upon an exclusive goal.
When the overwhelming drive for release is merged with the
still stronger drive for human intimacy, man rises to an
intensity and power far from the plodding isolation of much
of everyday experience. This power of emotional and physical
transcendence forms the foundation of the sex cults and
sexual mystiques, which also isolate and overemphasize these
experiences. Yet, interestingly enough, this transcendent
aspect of sexual pleasure closely matches the experiences of
God reported by contemplative mystics.

Many have speculated that the ecstasy which flickers so
quickly for man in sexual experiences will be the permanent
state of those who live with God in the new creation. This
joy and ecstasy of the resurrected, however, has been thought
of as beyond all forms of sexuality. C. S. Lewis projects the
image of a cosmic dance, a physical total participation beyond
sexuality. He postulates that pleasure in this eternal divine
dance would be as far above this life's sexual pleasure as
sexual pleasure now supersedes the pleasure of eating candy.
Others, too, have stressed the image of a soul's unity with
God which would completely transcend earthly sexual experience.

Those who insist that sexuality withers in heaven stress the
newness of the kingdom and quote Christ's words to the
effect that in "the resurrection men and women do not
marry; no, they are like the angels in heaven."[19] In Luke's

account the resurrected are called "sons of God," and Christ says of them that "they can no longer die" and of God that he is the "God of the living."[20] From these words, antisexual interpreters deduced everything from a theory that women could never be saved without first becoming men to the demand that to be saved one must not marry in this life either. At the opposite romantic extreme, Robert Browning could have a character in his *Ring and the Book* deduce from these words that to be like the angels might be *to be* married without being given in marriage, since the angels too may be coupled in angelic love.

Romantics to the contrary, the difficulty with human marriage from a heavenly point of view is its coupling exclusiveness. It takes a certain aggressiveness to choose and maintain a mating relationship. Even in all the variations of human custom from serial polygamy to polygamy, polyandry, or group marriage, there are some limits to the relationships, limits which are of necessity defended aggressively. Within humanity, intensity and commitment are accompanied by possessiveness; even Israel first knew Yahweh as a jealous God who demanded exclusive allegiance. In dimensions of ongoing time and contiguous space a choice of one action excludes the opposite. Even in sexual life outside marriage, no matter how hard man tries and some have tried valiantly, time, space, and the physical and nervous equipment of the body impose limits. If love and desire never fail, the heart eventually does; death finally frustrates man.

But the sons of the resurrection "can no longer die." The

limits we know of time and space no longer apply. Yet the testimony of Christ's resurrection implies that the new existence retains much continuity with the old. Personal identity remains in the glorified existence, but does this identity include sexual identity? The doctrine of the assumption of Mary precludes the notion that women need to become men first, but it says nothing of how important femininity itself is in the glorified state. However, since sexuality is an important way of human development and self-knowledge, it seems highly probable that male or female identity is transfigured and completed rather than superseded or suppressed. However, completed persons could not well be divided into the divisionary male-female oppositions of earth; as Paul says, "In Christ there is neither male nor female." The use of a common term such as "sons of the resurrection" or "sons of God" seems to indicate that common humanity and individual personality are ultimately far more important than sexual differentiation. Christ himself de-emphasized sexual and familial identity when he looked about him and said, "Whoever does the will of God is my mother, brother, sister."

Marriage and the exclusive relationship of the male-female couple can only be meaningful within the framework of limited time and space. Human procreation foreshadows the conquest of death, and it depends upon the two-sexed couple for genetic variability, specialized reproduction, and efficient long-term nurturing. However, without time, death, or need of the sexual differences evolved in time for the service of procreation, the couple no longer need be exclusive. As Christ taught, the wife married to seven brothers sequentially in this life can hardly belong to one of them exclusively forever. Particular belonging and the exclusive choice of marriage exist only when limitations are inevitable. Those "who do not die" neither marry nor are given in marriage; exclusive couplings of two-in-one-flesh unities cannot continue into new dimensions which supersede the time and space that create marriage and procreation.

To say, however, that there is no marriage in heaven is not the same thing as saying that there is no sexuality. A withering of sexuality in the absorbing God-man relationship is not the only alternative to marriage. The unique individual intimate Creator-created relationship will be an overwhelming joy of the new creation; but judging from Christ's witness, man's love of fellow men continues. If to love one another in this world is to love God, then communal relationships of man to man are all-important; and to have these horizontal human relationships perfected will be a supreme joy of the blessed. Man's social nature is so primary an aspect of his life and identity that salvation can only come as a species, a people, a community, a body. If one great means of relating to and loving others in life has been human sexuality, why should this wither in heaven? How gnostic to assume that "beyond time [sexuality] has no meaning," being only "a preparatory stage connected with procreation."[21]

If Christ promised a banquet in the kingdom, if speech and sight are fulfilled in love, then surely the primary human

sense of touch which gives self-identity, expresses so much
love, and gives so much pleasure would be fulfilled and completed. In this life married people can experience through
sexuality multidimensioned joy in knowing and loving another; perhaps this exclusive relationship prepares man for an
inclusive love and joy of all for all in the new life. There
would be no marriage of two-in-one-flesh in heaven, because
in an all-in-one-flesh community all would be married to all.
The coming of the kingdom is even described as the "marriage of the Lamb," a wedding of joy. With space and time
overcome, love for one another could be expressed tran-
scendently in all the ways of expressing love. In a transfigured
person all the individual's faculties and capacities would be
unified, and full communion with others would be possible.
With sexual identity transcended, the ecstasy of male-female
coupling could be expanded to all human relationships. The
prophets of a rescurrected body which is "polymorphously
perverse" might well expand their prophecy to include a body
generally genital as well.

The long history of Christianity has witnessed earlier
visions of a completed human sexuality in heaven. Such
theories, however, usually held at the same time other ideas
which were not only heretical but which, when practiced,
brought corruption and distortion to earthly Christianity.
Positive attitudes toward sexuality became tainted by erroneous, heretical principles. The usual difficulty, as with
some of the early Alexandrine Christian groups in their cele-
brations, was the assumption that uninhibited sexual liberty

could begin in this life.[22] Sexual promiscuity practiced in the name of Christian freedom denied any limitations in the human condition. Perfectionists and gnostic elites of one kind or another felt that man could disregard common human experience, the heritage of Jewish morality, and the Christian teaching that on earth man was to live in a monogamous male-female sexual relationship. These fringe groups, though often loudly proclaiming Christian inspiration in affirming sexuality, denied too much of the complete Christian message. Such truncated theologies, combined with pagan sexual excesses and gnostic influences, fueled antisexual bias among Christians through many centuries. Only recently have Christians regained their balance enough to start over again on sexual questions, to begin anew on a theology of sex. Questions of celibacy, sexual morality, marriage, procreation control, and family planning must all be reconsidered in the context of a newly balanced and affirmative Christian viewpoint.

In summary, Christians and others have erred when they have isolated human sexuality from man's personality as a whole or from the rest of human life. Both sexual mystiques and manichaean suspicions see human sexual experience as different from other human experiences, either especially dangerous or especially saving and revelatory of reality. Sexuality is, instead, one of the important ways to know one's self, to grow in potential, to relate to others. Sex is not more real or more important than other important human capacities such as speech, thought, or work. In fact, in the body-brain-consciousness unity of man, all of the human capacities are interrelated. Technical analysis of man or sex does not answer why man experiences pleasure from himself and his faculties. Sexual pleasure, being particularly intense and complex in humans, leads to questions of freedom, purpose, and man's joy in community.

Christians can recognize that human sexuality is a part of the good though incomplete creation of God. Sex, like all human faculties, reflects a God of love who joys in creation and community. The incarnation or enfleshment breaks through the Greek and pagan divisions of man and reality into "lower" bodies and "higher" souls. Love can no longer be disassociated from body or world. Christ the Whole, Holy One reconciles all divisions in his life, death, and resurrection. Christ's resurrection and continuing bodily life emphasize the dignity and importance of the embodied human person. Human processes have meaning and are important in bringing about the new creation, a kingdom in which love and joy reign. Pleasure, joy, play, violent ecstasy, and emotional expressions of the self through touch are gifts of God and as much a means of loving as sacrifice. Despite previous distortions of Christian thought, human sexuality is an important dimension of love and not alien to the Spirit. If human sexuality is to develop and bloom rather than wither away, our present sexual attitudes and behavior must be informed by a fully Christian view of sexuality, focused upon the triumph of the resurrection of the body.

NOTES

[1] Cf. Norman O. Brown, *Life against Death*, Vintage Books, New York, 1959; Brown, *Love's Body*, Random House, New York, 1966.

[2] Louis Bouyer, *The Seat of Wisdom*, tr. by A. Littledale, Pantheon Books, New York, 1962, p. 87.

[3] Dietrich von Hildebrand, *In Defense of Purity*, Helicon, Baltimore, 1962, pp. 75, 185.

[4] Paul M. Quay, S.J., "Contraception and Conjugal Love," *Theological Studies*, March 1961, p. 32.

[5] Karl Rahner, S.J., *Theological Investigations*, Vol. IV, Helicon, Baltimore, 1967, p. 245.

[6] Cf. Erik Erikson, *Insight and Responsibility*, Norton, New York, 1964.

[7] Cf. Harry Stack Sullivan, *Collected Works*, Norton, New York, 1965.

[8] Erik Erikson, *Childhood and Society*, 2nd ed., Norton, New York, 1963, p. 265.

[9] Leslie Farber, "I'm Sorry, Dear," *Commentary*, November 1964, p. 53.

[10] Paul Ricoeur, "Wonder, Eroticism, and Enigma," *Cross Currents*, Spring 1964, Vol. XIV, No. 2, p. 141.

[11] Quoted in Herbert Marcuse, *Eros and Civilization*, Vintage Books, New York, 1962, pp. 207-208.

[12] Sigmund Freud, *Sexuality and the Psychology of Love*, Collier Books, New York, 1963, p. 68.

[13] Helmut Thielicke, *The Ethics of Sex*, Harper, New York, 1964, p. 314.

[14] I Cor. 15:14-15.

[15] W. Pannenberg, *Grundzüge der Christologie*, Gütersloher Verlagshaus Gerd Mohn, Gütersloh, 1964, p. 79.

[16] Cf. Piet Schoenenberg, S.J., "The Real Presence in Contemporary Discussion," *Theology Digest*, Vol. XI, No. 1, p. 9; F. H. Drinkwater, "The Resurrection Appearances: Subjective or Objective?" *Continuum*, Winter-Spring 1967, Vo.l 5, No. 1, p. 181.

[17] Charles Davis, "This Jesus God Raised Up," *New Christian*, March 10, 1966.

[18] Luke 24:39-43.

[19] Matt. 22:30.

[20] Luke 20:36-38.

[21] Cf. Marc Oraison, *The Human Mystery of Sexuality,* Sheed and Ward, New York, 1967, pp. 170-171.

[22] Cf. John T. Noonan, *Contraception,* Harvard University Press, Cambridge, Mass., 1965, pp. 64, 67.

II

Celibacy: Affirmation of Freedom and Community

WITHIN ANY Christian reappraisal of sexuality, celibacy becomes an immediate issue. Can man live in celibacy? Should man live in celibacy? What about the value of sexuality and marriage? What about Christ? The tradition of Christian celibacy remains, and the institutional Church imposes celibacy on priests in the Latin rite. But more and more Roman Catholic Christians are questioning the law combining priesthood and celibacy, and it cannot be denied that the Church faces a celibacy crisis.

One of the first steps in inquiry consists of clearing away prevalent misconceptions. As seen in the previous chapter's discussion, problems in viewing sexuality arise from overestimation on the one hand and pessimistic alienation on the other. Mystique clashes with puritanical repugnance. In the mystique glorifying sexuality, celibacy is scorned and bludgeoned in the name of The Couple and salvation comes through heterosexual genitality. Ironically, the more naïve forms of this mystique often appear in the writing of male celibates who speak of Woman with a capital "W" and stress the organic unity and completion found in feminine and masculine unity. Old pagan ideas about the original man-woman, who being divided constantly seeks its other half for completion, influence these complaints against celibacy. Women are seen as embodying all the "eternal feminine" qualities, which they bestow upon their mates in marriage as they, in turn, receive completion from the male principle. This romantically naïve view of the glorious fulfillment of marriage seems closer to adolescent fantasy than to the marriage relationship between real men and real women, who always turn out to be human beings rather than "magic helpers."

A better understanding of sexuality and sexual identity among the Christian clergy and laity is imperative—for those who marry and for those who do not. Any system which miseducates and over-segregates young men and women can only result in poor marriages as well as many mistaken vocations to celibacy. Neither tabooed pessimism nor over-glorification prepares a person for human sexual relationships or for celibacy. It is essential in both cases to replace projections of fantasy with insights into the reality and complexity of human experience. Often it seems, outside the

Church as well as within it, sex, sexual identity, and marriage have to fill the void created by irrelevant work, stunted friendships, nonexistent community, a vague sense of the meaninglessness of the rest of life. The mystique of marriage and the couple which has failed so badly in the secular world would fall just as flat among a married clergy.

A more sophisticated but no less erroneous form of the couple mystique seeks to displace celibacy by founding its faith on the principle that personalities mature only through the couple's sexual relationship and experience. By denying himself or herself such relationship and experience with a beloved sexual partner, a person automatically stunts growth, self-knowledge, and contact with reality. Only through active, fully erotic love of another can man attain his destiny of infinite variety and growth. Married genital sexuality is so integral to personality growth that to suppress its expression in celibacy is dangerous and almost immoral. In this view, Christ's celibacy was unique; and any other celibates around who seem to have insight and maturity are puzzling and accidental exceptions to the rule.[1]

The basic fallacy of this view is not so much its bright faith in the saving power of genital sexuality (supported by some psychoanalysts and philosophers), but the way all reality extrinsic to the couple is ignored. Other things, other people, the larger community, work, family, art, misfortune—all have been squeezed out of the picture. The couple and their sexual activity exist in a void. One is reminded of the ancient pagan fertility cults where the copulation of the divine couple creates the world and keeps it going. In these modern versions of the myth, however, the aim of the couple is not "anonymous procreation," but "spiritual orgasms" which affirm unity, encounter, and identity through self-activity: the couple becomes the vehicle in which the Infinite Self flourishes. Obviously, then, celibates and others who are missing out on these "spiritual orgasms" cannot really develop as persons.

In crude contrast to such idealistic claims, the man-in-the-street version of the anticelibacy argument reduces sexuality to a matter of providing needed physical release, of Kinseyan "outlets" for sexual tensions. This diagnosis affirms simply that without sex people get "queer." Old maids, bachelors, and celibates develop typical eccentricities from sheer frustration. All they need is a bit of "you know what." Popularized Freudianism is sure that without sexual activity men and women are bound to become odd, narrow, and neurotic.

A compulsively coupled society, such as that which marks the contemporary American scene, degrades and despises single persons who are not sexually "fulfilled." Avid enthusiasts of Freud's libidinal theories are far less familiar with his ideas of sublimation, which are naturally less well publicized. Amidst all his dire warnings of dangers to the personality from frustration of the sexual instinct, Freud also described the specifically human process which he felt had kept culture and civilization intact: "This ability to exchange the originally sexual aim for another which is no longer sexual but is psychically related, is called the capacity for sublimation."[2] Freud maintained that this ability to sublimate the erotic drive differs among different humans depending upon their constitutional nature and the course of their development. The strong and healthy can wrest other satisfactions from the world, avoiding the unfortunate regressions that frustration can engender. Most natures, however, according to Freud, could not bear complete sexual frustration, although no person could attain to maturity without some frustration. Moreover, without some degree of frustration and inhibition, people could not live together and civilization could not exist.

If sublimation or "long-circuiting of energy" is possible in a Freudian analysis of sexuality based on life-forces and instinctual energy, it is all the more feasible when personalist elements of sexuality are emphasized. Human sexuality is a dimension of self-consciousness and a way in which the individual seeks contact, community, and communication with others. The infant receives pleasure from his sense contact with outer reality, and the developing body organizes this pleasure in a continuing contact and communication that moves progressively toward the final focus on genitality and generativity. This whole process parallels and participates in a similar ego development, as well as in mental and social development. Each stage of development includes giving up a former satisfaction to avoid fixation and taking on a more complicated, more highly organized, more other-centered satisfaction with more social implications. During the course of this progressive development, one "sublimates," or con-

verts or takes up, the energy and pleasure of each stage of
development into the next stage—living a series of "graduations," as Erikson puts it.[3] The law of the process seems to
be that if you do not keep growing, you regress and de-
generate. Infantilism in the noninfant is far different from
infantilism in original physical infancy. In health and maturity the personality keeps expanding in its capacity for love,
for work, for the further development of one's self and one's
community.

Except for the obvious denial by confirmed pansexualists,
agreement comes from most observers that the process of
personal growth can keep operating in persons who lead lives
of sexual abstinence. Many such persons do not regress, but
continue the process of converting erotic energy into communal love and work. Their responsiveness and cooperation
with others keeps them sensitive, alert, and fulfilled. As long
as the physical desire for love and unity can be sublimated
into friendship, charity, and service, as long as the physical
and creative tension can be spent in creative work, the personality keeps expanding. Conversely, a couple's superb
sexual loving relationship does not necessarily guarantee
personality expansion. Some ten thousand orgasms over the
course of a marriage do not necessarily change the personalities. The life lived between and beyond sexual encounters
determines not only the couple's sexuality but also their
personality growth. Man can live with sex or without it, but
he can't do without community life and expression. Old

maids and bachelors get "that way" when they cut themselves off from growth through nonparticipation in community life, not because they sleep alone.

Freud appears correct; it seems that the unique human capacity to displace sexual drive and energy to other efforts has built human culture, community, and civilization. The richer the communal culture, the intellectual level, and the civilization, the more access an individual has to the community—and the less deprivation there is in sexual abstinence. In an impoverished, shallow culture with no access to art, literature, tradition, intellect, religion, athletics, work, or communal life (such as that of the Puerto Rican slum dwellers described by Oscar Lewis in *La Vida*), sexual abstinence would be almost impossible. Often the only expression and fulfillment open to those deprived of everything else is genital sexuality, which in its turn is distorted by the conditions of community life. In contrast, every rich, developed culture has included celibates—usually, as in the case of Hindu Brahmins and Zen Buddhists, in the role of religious leader. So too, warriors and students, living in close community and expending high levels of energy in work, have often been celibate.

At another extreme of experience, the fact that drug addicts and natural mystics are almost invariably sexually abstinent complicates the question of celibacy. In these cases the pregenital state of infancy is regained (or regressed to, according to one's value judgment) through chemical means or naturally occurring psychic states of euphoria. The genital drive, with its pleasurable violence, possessiveness, impetus toward the opposite sex, and its social direction toward future procreation, is not even desired. Comfort, peace, and delight are found in a present perception of natural phenomena, in an oceanic oneness with all matter and all sensation. The confrontation with the particular physical reality and the specific desire implicit in human sexual intercourse cannot compete with the soaring inclusive delights of the psychic experience. The totality of the "trip" or the "immersion in light" makes exclusive, specific sexual pleasure seem too limited.

In those who are chemically addicted, however, there is a passive response to the concrete outer community. No sublimation of energy takes place, but rather a withdrawal into apathy. From a social point of view, this form of isolated apathetic celibacy can only be seen as a regression analogous to the sexual disinterest accompanying physical disease. Celibacy, to be meaningful for the person and society, must be the sublimated kind; it must be a celibacy that passes through the sexual maturity of desire and genitality, not beneath, around, over, or below it (to use some questionable imagery). Infantile pregenital celibacy which has either never reached or radically renounces identity, individuality, purpose, focus, organization, and the future cannot be a Judeo-Christian goal. Norman O. Brown's "polymorphously perverse" resurrected body is no body at all; man cannot aspire to be a communally dreaming animal.[4]

An important and relevant distinction in psychic life between denial and suppression should be noted here. Denial involves the nonacceptance of something, even in the face of obvious evidence, while suppression means the conscious rejection of a recognized impulse, thought, or desire. Denial is dangerous, suppression invaluable. Once suppression is chosen, sublimation can be effected, unlike total denial wherein all processes become paralyzed. Meaningful celibacy must be based upon suppression and sublimation of mature sexual desire and capacity, not on denial or incapacity. Just as one's own dim history of incest wishes and unacceptable desires can be faced and suppressed in the process of achieving free maturity, other sexual desires and inclinations should be recognized as arising naturally. Shock, denial, frantic resistance to one's own sexuality, always makes matters worse and impede the sublimation that allows robust friendship to bloom across sexual divisions.

One can manage all kinds of healthy friendships without denial of sexuality. Although friendships within one's own sex do include a potential homosexual relationship, this possibility repudiates accepted sexual identities and cultural norms. It is therefore strongly inhibited, and the very strength of this inhibition normally makes friendships within one's own sex relaxed and easy. Friendship with members of the opposite sex, however, includes much more sexual potential; a whole new merged future, reaching even to future descendants, hovers over the present. This potential for a new world of pleasure and procreation provides the extra emotional stimulation in relationships between the sexes. The stimulation increases as the person of the opposite sex matches personal preferences in matters of looks, age, emotional compatibility, and intellectual ideals. This extra dimension gives zest to social life and resonance to friendship.

The point to be stressed is that participation in these emotional colorations gives more to the individual and society than denial or timid flight into rigid segregation of the sexes. Unspoken mutual renunciation can give a certain edge to relationships that other friendships lack. To recognize barriers and yet to affirm and go beyond them through sublimation can be a good working principle for the celibate (and the married) in relationships in which sexual expression is inappropriate. In a culture that knows so much about man's emotional reactions, it is not necessary to control sexuality with means like the severe avoidance techniques of some primitive tribes in which men never speak to some women or in which the male and female language may even be different. Surely Christ's condemnation of "lust" for a neighbor's wife alluded to an exploitative emotion consciously held for a long period of time, not spontaneous desires which are calmly and immediately suppressed. Spontaneous sexual desire simply proves that we are human, healthy, and emotionally alive.

With irrational guilt out of the way, it can be liberating to realize that emotional attraction is the basis of all friendship and love. Of course, genital love within the life commitment of marriage is probably the most intense giving possible, with the exception of the sacrifice of life for love of another. Successful celibates are those who have the capacity for reciprocal love in marriage and yet can give their love and life in other ways. Once the genital potential and ego maturity necessary for marriage is there, sublimation can work for those with the capacity to endure and go beyond frustration. It is those with a stable, loving, joyous nature who do best in the celibate state, for it is the strong and secure self who can most easily establish community in other ways, who can give and receive love without the confirmation and release of sexual consummation.[5]

This discussion of celibacy has thus far applied to any celibate, to those who are frustrated by circumstance as well as those who would voluntarily choose the state. Choosing celibacy for religious reasons as a conscious vocation involves more complex concerns. One of the problems has been that the old ideal of Christian celibacy incorporated negative and inadequate thinking about sexuality and man. Dedicated virginity came to be praised and practiced for the wrong reasons. One of the most prevalent of all the mistaken motivations for male celibacy has been the fear of contamination by women. Pagan spiritualism found all flesh dangerous, with woman's very fleshy flesh worst of all. Gnostic influences and the Old Testament heritage of woman's danger and uncleanness arising from her sexuality were developed in patristic times into a bitter hostility toward women. Dedicated virginity for men almost became as much a way of avoiding women and sexuality as it was of serving God. Happily, remnants of this whole sick syndrome are increasingly rare. Nevertheless, fear, dread, and the avoidance of sexuality as defilement have done much to discredit the vocation of virginity and to stunt many of those, both men and women, who chose this vocation.

Another related distortion has been the idea of dedicated virginity as the consecration to God of an undefiled and perfect body. This emphasis upon the purity of the offering includes an exaggerated concern with the maintenance of physical virginity. The basis of this old theme, that the offerings in the temple must not have spot nor blemish, leads right back to the pagan suspicion of sexuality as contamination. Purification themes cannot be well integrated into a Christian affirmation of the creation, or of procreation and sexuality. The physical criterion that the body, or rather the genitalia, not be touched, used, or violated misses the point that the body is being presented as a living sacrifice (emphasis upon "living"). Hyper-concern with purity and the genital sacrifice reflects the pagan overestimation and isolation of sexuality from life. When the world is thought to have been created by divine coitus instead of fiat, phallic concerns are magnified. The vestal virgins were in a sense totems for the tribe, and all attention was focused on their physical purity, not on other aspects of their identity. Remnants of this magical enhancement and awe of physical purity must disappear in Christian thought, just as any equally pagan suspicion and scorn of celibacy must go. Over-sacralization of sexuality is merely a defense that fear imposes; it has no place in the Christian view of persons, love, and creation.

Another overworked, unsatisfactory image, that of the celibate's "marriage to God," also belongs to the pagan syndrome. Fertility gods and goddesses require special sexual responses from humanity—either sexual sacrifice or temple prostitution or ritual fertility rites to make the crops grow. Again, sexuality becomes preeminent in life when it should be only important. In the Christian form of this pagan pansexualism, the sexual imagery in the Old Testament and the New is isolated and exaggerated so that the theme of Christ as bridegroom and "the marriage of the Lamb" is applied directly to the individual vocation of virginity. But can one really take scriptural imagery and examples in parables, isolate them, and transmute them into the theory of an individual marriage to God lived in virginity? This is dubious logic and gives rise to many corruptions of Christian thought. The couple mystique, so damaging to marriage, is worse when applied to Christ and an individual. Instead of seeing the bridal imagery as common to all Christians and as an endorsement of human sexual love, a terrible dichotomy appears. A Jesuit can write even in the 1960's: "In the state of fallen nature man finds it especially difficult not to prejudice the love of God by marital love," followed by "it is more precious to give all one's love to God than to share it with a human being."[6] Such separation of the love of God from the love of human beings goes completely against the central message of the New Testament, and belies the use of sexual imagery as well.

Even the command to "hate" wife and family in order to

follow Christ, a command that seems so harsh despite meta-
phoric interpretation, came from the Christ who insisted that
following him meant obeying the central commandment:
Love one another. There could be no authentic love of God
or Christ that did not manifest itself in love of humans.
The idea that "a spiritual marriage union gives the love of
God that exclusiveness which is the essential basis of the
objective priority of virginitas over marriage" almost blas-
phemes by asserting that to exclude other people could be
proper in one's love for God.[7] Christ reserved his strongest
condemnations for those who taught that love of God excluded love of man; and John, himself the "beloved disciple,"
made the love of man the proof of love for God. To separate
and isolate love of God or to consider that it competes with
love of man distorts Christianity. This strange contradiction
of Christian doctrine can only have been applied to celibacy
because of the gnostic tendency to detach sexuality from love
and the rest of human life and to see sexuality as particularly
open to sinful influence. Since marital love included sexuality, it had to be different from love of God or love of neighbor, different in kind. God was somehow absent from, if not
displeased by, sexuality; love pleasing to God reigned only
from the waist up.

All of the angelic-life parallels accorded to celibacy are also
inadequate. They, too, gnostically assume unreconciled spirit-
body divisions in which men choosing to live like angels must
emphasize their higher, spiritual capacities at the expense
of their lower, fleshy body. These theories assume too much

inside information about angels and exhibit great ignorance of the reality of man's complex personal unity. Angelic ideals for man not only counter the example of the incarnation but deny the resurrection of the body. Without a conviction of the continuity of loves in human development and with little penetration of the full meaning of the incarnation, Christians kept separating physical and spiritual love. To seek pleasure and union in the married couple's sexual relationship was condemned by implication if not by fact, while a far more self-centered, individualistic ideal of spiritual marriage to God, complete with mystical ecstasy, favors, and comforts, was thought exemplary.

This exclusiveness and selfish concentration on solitary salvation through individual heavenly betrothal distorts the vocation of virginity. Christ the Bridegroom came for the whole Church and is not to be selfishly thought of as an individual's spouse. In Christ's promise of unity with his followers, he reassures them that "he who loves me will be loved by my Father"; in his priestly prayer for unity, he prays to the Father that "all may be one in us." The "marriage of the Lamb" is an inclusive communal affair, not a private couple-centered ceremony. Besides, the nonsexual images of shepherd, friend, king, judge, bread, vine, light, gate, sonship, adoption, and brotherhood are equally appropriate to describe human beings in their I-we-Thou relationships to Christ.

Emphasizing bridal imagery has too often been unfortunate, especially in the case of young women dedicating themselves to celibacy. The image of the bride, rather than emphasizing the communal marriage covenant, has been used to further feminine passivity and modest shrinking from earthy realities. The Christian ideal of becoming "sons of God who overcome" with "the liberty of the sons of God" has too often been entangled in veils, too often smothered by sentiment. The euphoria encouraged by viewing oneself as an individually chosen bride distorts the Christian life. It is almost a miracle that a saint like Thérèse of Lisieux could achieve sanctity in a vocation of virginity despite the cloying sentiment and bad theology of her milieu. As Thérèse passed from viewing a snowfall as a present from heaven on her wedding day to grim endurance of anxiety, her sanctity grew. Even in her confining circumstances and culture her realization of the Church as a horizontal community of commitment and human love rescued her from self-centered sentimental piety. Again and again in Christian history, vocations of celibacy have been distorted by themes of exclusiveness, purification, angelism, and denial.

Far better motivations and deductions sustain the true Christian ideal of dedicated virginity. Perhaps first and foremost in any reappraisal is the affirmation that celibacy is a vocation of inclusiveness rather than exclusiveness. This basis seems the best reading of Christ's words on the subject. When Christ said that some eunuchs make themselves so for the sake of the kingdom, the emphasis should be on "for the sake of the kingdom of heaven." The celibate, one "who can accept this," becomes the communal man, dedicated to the community of the kingdom. The love of God and man, to which every Christian is called whatever his vocation, can be lived by the communal man in complete dedication to the Christian community and the world at large.

The communal man gives up an individual family as well as house and lands in order to create a more inclusive family; he gives up an individual mate to be able to love many more intensely and fully. Just as each person in the course of his development must be frustrated and so "graduate" from love of parents to mature heterosexual love, so some give up freely the love of a mate and children for love of many. As the incest taboo forces individuals to create new families and social groups through extending kinship ties, so a voluntary frustration of the genital drive helps create an extended and inclusive human family beyond primary biological identity and kinship. Dedicated celibacy can be seen as a voluntary barrier assumed for the sake of creating a new universal family, a new inclusive relationship to humanity. After all, only after the child gives up complete physical possession of the beloved in his family can he turn to the work of the world and begin to love others in the larger community. Celibacy, like the incest taboo, expels the individual from the immediate satisfactions of the known family community to found and find new human relationships. The possessiveness and desire for complete physical expression of unity that informs mature human love can be sublimated. The vocation to virginity is a free, self-imposed obstacle to sexual fulfill-

ment and self-expression in order to provoke wider sublimations and more inclusive loyalties.

Celibacy as a sacrificial suppression of mating for the sake
of extending the family relationship to every member of one's
own and the opposite sex creates both an inclusive unity
and an expanded freedom for the development of mankind.
The prohibition against genital sexual expression and the
promise to maintain the barrier can give a freedom and availability to all human relationships: a radical freedom to give.
The dedicated celibate should be the completely available
one, with emotional energy completely devoted to the community. His or her talents and efforts are focused on building
the kingdom. The complete gift of the celibate's time, energy,
and love can be made without taking anything from others.
The renunciation of property, home, and even of life, can be
made without injuring the welfare of others. Those who scorn
St. Paul's remark about the conflicting loyalties imposed by
marriage might meditate upon the suffering wives and children of two great married martyrs: Thomas More and Franz
Jägerstätter. Their martyrdoms of conscience were compounded and complicated by the suffering of their de-
pendents.

The question of sacrifice brings us to another motivation
for dedicated virginity; it is a lived affirmation of a Christian view of reality. And a vital part of that reality is the
recognition that martyrdom may be required in the struggle
for the kingdom-to-come. Christ promised persecution to his
followers, and our own American peace and civil rights

martyrs prevent us from smugly dismissing martyrdom as far away and long ago. In a time of conflict and struggle the readiness to lay down one's life for the community can come more easily to those whose decision can be made alone. Celibacy, along with poverty, is a sign of a willing death of the individual for the group life. The larger family of man assumes the place of actual progeny and family—this is a death-in-life sacrifice of the immediate for the kingdom-to-come, the seen for the unseen. Dedicated virginity in its willingness to live and die for God and the total community can become a way of reconciling the apartness and divisions in the world. Even without sin, the categories of time and space frustrate human community since procreation and childbearing impose exclusive and primary loyalties. Forgetting for the moment the evil choices which are made, good choices often cancel other good choices. The Christian hope is that all these necessary limitations, discontinuities, misfortunes, and conscious rejections of good in man's history are reconciled in Christ's resurrection whereby he, the Alpha and the Omega, inaugurates the new creation.

Somehow, Christ Resurrected is able to be completely available and present to many simultaneously. Limitations imposed by our categories of time and space no longer have power over him. For us, however, in this life, while we still await the fulfillment of the parousia, individual and communal completion can conflict. What's good for one may not be good for all. The individual Christian chooses to go through the exclusive procreative relationship of the couple to the community or, more rarely, through sacrifice of the married relationship to availability and service to all. Until the completion and fulfillment of the kingdom in the parousia, Christians are faced with limiting choices. Those who choose the married relationship live the sign of completeness, of restored creation, fullness, joy—"all things are yours." Those who choose dedicated celibacy live the sign of incompleteness, of fulfillment to come, of aspiration to a more complete community and perfect unity.

Celibacy proclaims the assertion and hope for the reality of a completed history when God will be all in all. Perhaps the reason some Christian celibates arouse more than their share of resentment from some of today's racist mobs, as well as from past and present and totalitarian regimes, is exactly because the affirmation of hope implicit in their life choice proclaims that the world community is incomplete, that now is not enough, that the status quo will not satisfy. The celibate's freely chosen sacrifice, for the sake of the present and the future of the kingdom, witnesses to the reality of a community which cannot be encompassed or distinctly envisioned. In this sense, Christian celibacy *is* "foolishness." Only those with a strong conviction of the kingdom's reality, of the full meaning of the resurrection, could bear the cost of such "foolish" sacrifice.

Consider the testimony of a former German officer ruefully commenting on his dilemma in the war, on why he and his fellows had not attempted some form of protest against an S.S. unit that was killing Jews in Sevastopol: "None of us had a conviction so deeply rooted that we would have taken upon ourselves a practically useless sacrifice for the sake of a higher moral meaning."[8] A sacrifice that is "practically useless" (viewed in the context of the individual and his life-span) witnesses to faith and confers moral authority. Radical renunciation of personal power through poverty, chastity, and obedience affirms Christian belief. Celibacy, as one aspect of the evangelical life, asserts God's power to bring life from death, community from loneliness, family from renounced procreation. Men trust Christ's words, and believe that the seed that dies will bloom and bear fruit. Married Christians do this too and daily die to selfishness in other ways; but if Christ had lied or been mistaken in his message, marriage and procreation would be the only way that man could make the most of his human condition. If there is no living Christ, no kingdom transcending death, he who has left all has lost all forever. Only in this sense of a more clear manifestation of Christian hope and a more complete dependence upon God's power can celibacy be considered superior to marriage. Marriage is superior in its fuller expression of human sexuality; celibacy, however, by sacrificing sexual exclusiveness, foreshadows the heavenly condition of all being married to all. But it is a waste of time to speculate on the comparative merits of the different ways to God when everything is dependent upon the personality and circumstances of the individual who must do the choosing. "Each has his gift," says St. Paul, despite his personal feeling that with the imminence of Christ's second coming celibacy was preferable.

Christ himself seems to have made distinctions and recognized different vocations. Some hearers of his words were asked to give up all and physically follow him around the countryside; others were told to begin their new life in the kingdom while remaining where they were, in their married state, in their same social occupation. Throughout the ministry in which he preached radical sacrifice of all things, Christ also affirmed marriage, family love, and the just use of property and power. But many have wondered that Christ gave so little explicit teaching on both celibacy and man's sexuality. This so-called silence and the lack of explanation of his own celibate example have been variously interpreted.

Those of one tradition consider it unthinkable that Christ should have been anything but celibate. In this older gnostic view, abstinence from the contamination of sexuality and desire would be the minimum requirement for any holy man, much less a God-man. Therefore, silence about Christ's sexuality springs from the fact that such speculations are basically unmentionable. For those spiritualist minds so dominant for much of Christian history, the problem instead revolves around the justification of marriage and any use of sexuality as without sin. At the extreme opposite pole are those who interpret Christ's lack of explicitness as a sign that Christ lived as other men, either having been married before his ministry or living in a sexual relationship with Mary Magdalene; but such suggestions usually come from those who know little of scripture or the Jewish milieu and tradition in which Christ lived. Still another variant of the pro-marriage, pro-sexual interpretation of Christ's life, while not questioning Christ's celibacy, interprets it as a unique adjunct of his divinity which, like his birth, cannot be an example for his followers.

A more pertinent approach seems to view the relative silence of Christ on sexuality as a purposeful way to demonstrate the neutrality of sexuality in a pagan world suffused with sexual mystique and a religious world suffering from fearful sexual avoidance.[9] As God calmly created sexuality in the Genesis story as one of the good things of creation (denying pagan sexual creation stories), so Christ's calm, integrated attitude confirmed the creation story and began Christianity's demythologizing of sexuality. Christ affirmed marriage, affirmed celibacy, by word and example for the sake of the kingdom. The omission of many specific discussions and teachings on sexuality assumed a sexuality that was integrated into life, not a special focus of sin needing a special morality. His contemporaries wondered that he taught with such integrated authority; but what seems wonderful to us, in our disassociated unease, is the integrity and self-assurance of his love of men and women. He spoke with women, traveled with them, had special friendships with them, and without losing poise in the midst of a gathering of learned enemies could have a fallen woman weep tears upon his feet and dry them with her hair. So too, Jesus could embrace John, the much-loved disciple, as naturally as he could weep over Lazarus' death.

Unfortunately, imitating Christ in any of these relationships with men and women would probably incur grave
censure from most spiritual directors of young celibates. One
wonders about the source of a "Christian" mandate that results in immediate panic at the very thought of emotional,
special friendships—as if there could be any other kind of
friendship. Surely, it is an odd triumph of old heresies to
keep denying to Christians the characteristics found in Christ
and the great Christian saints who tenderly loved their special friends of both sexes without stinting on other loving. A
sense of great love and physical tenderness pervades all of
Christ's inclusive and special relationships with men, women,
and children. He is friend, shepherd, the mother hen with
her chicks, the gentle firstborn elder brother. Yet the consum-
ing fire of passion is reserved for his commitment and work
for the kingdom. Christ's celibacy is directly connected with
his devotion to the kingdom and his freedom for complete
giving to all unto death. No repugnance for the body's involvement in sexual processes is implied in his celibacy; after
all, fetal existence, infancy, work, suffering, and death incorporated Christ totally into the human condition. He loved,
created a community, and gave himself for it completely.
But his consummation was communal, one to draw all men
to him. We can say of Christ, as we can of many of his
celibate followers: What more could marriage have done for
him or he for marriage? Following Christ's example of celibacy for the kingdom is a valid way of love for those Christians "to whom it is given." For Christian celibacy, as exem-

plified in Christ's own life, witnesses not only to human limitation and sin through renunciation, but it also—and basically—witnesses to the Christian hope and belief in the primacy of community beyond kinship through inclusive love.

Moreover, this witness, like Christ's life, can effectively demythologize sexuality and can free personal identity and function to go beyond male and female identities and roles. St. Paul says that "in Christ there is neither male nor female, Jew nor Greek, slave nor free, but all are one in Christ." Unity transcending primary sexual identities can only be achieved in this world by renunciation—however different all this might be for the sons of the resurrection who no longer die. Current polarity mystiques of male-female encounter in exclusive pairs must give way to a higher view of human identity: the individual person completed in God and the human community. With the end of sexual polarity, men will be freed from the masculine mystique of virility, dominance, and aggression (the old Latin ideal of *machismo*); women will gain a recognition of their value as human beings apart from giving men pleasure and producing progeny.

Both men and women progress to a richer maturity when personality development is not hampered by sexual stereotypes of "feminine" and "masculine" natures. Labeling human qualities and virtues either "male" or "female" stunts human beings from growing "into the fullness of Christ." The practice of celibacy affirms that being a human being is much more important than one's initial identity as a male or female. The tradition of those in religious life taking names from the opposite sex has countered the confining of personal identities and roles to polarized sexual ones. There is far more to the body-person than heterosexuality and genitality. Sexual polarization of the human race has been damaging in many ways, to both men and women, even to sexual pleasure and functioning in marriage. In a masculine-dominated world, however, women particularly have suffered and been suppressed in the name of the supposed vast sexual differences between male and female functioning. The ideal of Christian celibacy which stresses that "the body is for the Lord" frees both men and women for a more mature and expansive development—a development of self and of relationship to the community apart from specific genital relationships.[10]

Value beyond sexual identity also validates those humans without eugenic value or procreative potential: the young, the old, the sick and deformed. When human beings are thought of as primarily productive or reproductive, those who do not produce or reproduce are demeaned. Genital relationships are extremely productive—of pleasure, progeny, psychic comfort. They are thoroughly oriented to reciprocal fulfillment in the pragmatic present. Celibacy, with its sacrifice for the future, is thoroughly nonpragmatic and a one-way form of giving. Christian affirmation of the nonproductive, nonfulfilled, "useless" human being protects and validates those who cannot be living in productive genital reciprocity.

The ideal of Christian celibacy also gives freedom to a culture by providing an openness that delivers the individual person from the closed, limiting identities of sex, tribe, and role. Only options and alternatives give free choice. Even marriage relationships can only achieve their own transcendence in love and personal unity when each member possesses further loyalties to more extended communities and ideals beyond pleasure or personal love and procreation. When marriage and/or sexual fulfillment becomes mandatory for everyone, personal elements of choice and freedom deteriorate. Cultures in which celibate priests and men and women religious are uncomprehended or despised as half human often have a similarly inadequate ideal of the person, especially of women as persons. In such cultures marriage is not seen as a free personal relationship. Marriage and sexuality flourish best when seen as a relative rather than an encompassing reality, as David Burrell rightly stresses in discussing the complementary interrelationship of marriage and celibacy.[11]

Options for singleness and dedicated celibacy bespeak a developed community, and vocations to celibacy within the Christian community are as necessary as prophecy. Woe to us as a Christian community when no one becomes celibate for the sake of the kingdom.

This brings us face to face with the present Christian community's decreasing numbers of those choosing the evangelical life. This accelerating decrease, however, does not necessarily herald woe and disaster. Considering the history of the present rigid forms of religious life and the accumulation of distorted views of celibacy, the present loss of celibate vocations may be but a sign of renewal. How many of our present religious communities reflect but the lack, rather than the witness, of inclusive love and freedom to serve the kingdom? And the imposition of clerical celibacy on the secular priesthood does seem an arbitrary law more concerned with conformity than with mission and witness to the world, much less with new psychological insights into personality development and human sexuality. The non-evangelical burdens of finances, property, and organization might well be "lightened" for many parish priests by marriage, while those most needful of family experiences might well be bishop-administrators. Pope Paul VI has admitted that celibacy and the priesthood do not necessarily imply each other, only that the law is more fitting. But, unhappily, "fitting" witness of celibacy is still viewed as witness of exclusiveness in loving God, a concept degrading to human sexual love. Obviously the Church needs a lightning-paced evolution of ideals incarnated in practical flexibility and freedom. Still the celibacy crisis is not so drastic as some of the other current crises—birth control and authority, for example—because the theological issues are less confused and reform can be merely a matter of the Church changing its laws. If there is no change and vocations keep decreasing, the Church will simply become more lay controlled and lay led, with a natural and corresponding lessening of clerical influence and emphasis. Pope Paul's firm stand against a married clergy may mean the beginning of a new-style Church.

A great problem in this time of transition, however, is the Church's attitude toward the present difficulties of those in celibate vocations. All know that celibacy for the secular priesthood is a matter of law rather than revelation, and many celibates can see that their own prior conditioning by the Church's inadequate theology kept them from making mature Christian decisions and promises. Should present insights into themselves, into sexuality, and into a fuller Christian theology always be sacrificed to their past immature decisions? Now that the Church is teaching a new appreciation of potential service in the world, both in the lay state and in marriage, it is not surprising that many of today's celibates feel that their previous promise was not a free one. Now that it is understood that choosing between marriage and celibacy is a choice between two good vocations, it can hardly be called base infidelity to choose an alternate way to love and serve God and man. Promises and fidelity to structures do keep mankind going—but so does growth and the courage to change. Surely some flexible concessions and channels can be arranged to get the community through this time of change in Christian attitudes.

It is particularly misleading in argument to compare the promise of celibacy to the promise in a marriage relationship. Once the marriage relationship is established, any alternate choice means deserting a spouse (and often children), but a former celibate's marriage does not "hurt" God or "diminish" the Church unless the Church arbitrarily cuts off his membership and rejects his service. Marriage is a human right, a gift from God, a way to sanctity. Only the older misguided mystique of the sexually undefiled sacrificial virgin, of celibacy viewed as "marriage to God," could use images of adultery to describe the marriage of a formerly celibate secular priest. This reaction is like that of the Romans who killed any vestal virgin who had become "sexually contaminated," and it indicates emotional failure in coming to terms with human sexuality. Even in the past those married couples without the responsibility of children who made mutual decisions to enter religious orders were not condemned. To change the form and expression of Christian love and commitment within the community seems but a valid response to changing human beings and their changing human needs.

True, as cannot be said too often, promise and commitment keep culture and civilization intact through man's acceptance of responsibility for his own future. It may be a bit discouraging to see that a person has been mistaken and has not been able to shape himself and his life as he once desired. However, commitment to a particular role within the community follows individual capacity to function, so roles should remain flexible as long as no one else's welfare is involved. The movement to seminaries for delayed vocations takes account of human change, and so does the establishment of a married deaconate and the ordaining of married men who have been ministers and priests before becoming

Catholics. Yet suggestions for renewable vows, giving secular priests the option to marry, and freer transition from religious vocations to the lay married state continue to meet staunch opposition.

Vestiges of myths surrounding Church government and authority combine with sexual mystiques to maintain the image of the priest as a sacred person, as set aside from mankind, different from other men. The priest as ministering brother disappears; the pagan priest-king rather than Christ becomes the operating model. A demythologized Christian maturity about authority and sexuality should be able to welcome celibate vocations within the Christian community at the same time that married pregnant women priests (to take the most discomforting opposite extreme) would not be thought offensive. The Church needs sexual witness to the immanence and transcendence of God and the kingdom in every various form the community can provide. The Roman Catholic mold for clergy, in contrast, has generally segregated young priests-to-be, creating for them a small separate world with its own law, language, economy, advancement, and etiquette. By the time these young men have become the old men who govern and hold the power in the system, they have lost touch with much of the world at large and many of their fellow Christians.

Granted that a certain amount of segregation may be necessary for formation of any kind, prolonged segregation by age and/or sex seems dangerous. In particular, groups of adult one-sex societies tend toward fancy dress, pomposity,

verbosity, ritualism, and irrelevancy as though these were
necessary compensations for the stimulus that a variety of
age, sex, and family relationships might give to the group.
Requirements of maleness and celibacy for all the priesthood cut off too much human experience to Church leadership and function. Could the curia and the local diocesan
imitations of the Roman bureaucracy be quite so cold, petty,
and legalistic with the presence of men and women priests,
married and celibate priests, ministering couples, wives, children, and grandchildren? Such variety could bring some of
the flexible, fluid vitality of the apostolic Church into our
existing bureaucracies.

Imposed institutionalized total celibacy, which may have
served well in the past, may be only one symptom of the
rigidity of the crumbling *Romanità* style in our world, but it
is a major one symbolically. The Church must now show its
acceptance of sexuality, marriage, and love for the world
and persons in concrete ways of freedom, flexibility, and
participation in human life. An institution we must have;
structure, priesthood, apostolic succession, and vocations of
celibacy we must have. But to close the priesthood to all but
males with a celibate vocation is to force the Spirit who blows
where he listeth into a narrow corridor indeed. Many in the
Roman tradition who can readily see the suffering and loss
in Protestant Christian communities that have denied the vocation of celibacy are contrastingly blind to the fact that
Rome has also been deprived by its own rigidity. One of the
most obvious results of rigidity is the appearance of what

one priest calls "biased intake."[12] When there is no freedom
and no viable choice, those who can aspire to the priesthood
can include only those who have already made up their minds
to celibacy (often at a dangerously young age, at that). But
the main problem with the lack of options and freedom is
the damage done to the continuing vocation of celibacy.

Celibacy, for both men and women, can only be meaningful as a free choice of love and service to the community
for the sake of the kingdom. Since it is a hard way to live
and love, it should be chosen freely, not forced by law. If a
person finds that he can no longer intensely love and serve
many, then far better that he or she renew their loving with a
mate and family. Christ commanded us to love one another,
and nothing is more vital in our Christian life. Those "who
can" are able to serve and love the whole community; most
men and women need the concrete demands and reciprocity
of mate and family to grow in love. Sexual love and parenthood force human confrontation and human giving and receiving; celibates must be able to freely create other forms of
care and human community. Fully mature Christians,
whether married or celibate, seem to reach the same goals of
self-integrity and sensitive giving to others, but the celibate
vocation seems to contain more risks of withering into selfish
isolation. An exploitative use of marriage often made love
and growth in marriage difficult in the past; today, unfortunately, the living conditions, parish structures, and institutional mediocrity suffered by many celibates make living and

growing in their communal vocation even more difficult. Freedom to choose, freedom to change, and freedom to grow are absolutely necessary for celibacy in the Church.

Knowing and growing is difficult for all, but those who give up the ready-made intimacy, confrontations, and joys of family life have to fling themselves into other ways of community and human relationship. Only thus can the Christian celibate witness to the importance of a community beyond biological ties, to personality and pleasures beyond the sexual, to a future fulfillment completing this life beyond death. By relinquishing a most certain way of knowing and loving and procreating a family, the celibate for the sake of the kingdom proclaims the validity of all other ways to knowledge and community. By sacrificing sexual relationship with one, the celibate opens himself to all, to the creation of an inclusive family. Instead of using the old imagery of marriage to God, a better imagery would speak of marriage to each and every human being—with special commitment to those in the weakness of youth, age, poverty, illness, to those who do not have the support and love of a mate or family. By denying a one-flesh unity with another, the celibate prepares for the future one-flesh unity of all with all. He witnesses in hope to the power of God to bring strength from weakness, oneness from separateness, joy from sorrow, life from death. In a very real way the ideal of Christian celibacy frees and expands the idea of man. Man is the free species who can freely choose his destiny, who can freely create community.

NOTES

[1] Cf. Dan Sullivan, "Celibacy and the Contraception Debate," *National Catholic Reporter,* August 17, 1966.

[2] Sigmund Freud, *Sexuality and the Psychology of Love,* Collier Books, New York, 1963, p. 26.

[3] Cf. Erik Erikson, *Childhood and Society,* 2nd ed., Norton, New York, 1963.

[4] Cf. Norman O. Brown, *Life against Death,* Vintage Books, New York, 1959.

[5] Cf. Marc Oraison, *The Celibate Condition and Sex,* Sheed and Ward, New York, 1967.

[6] Wilhelm Bertrams, S.J., *The Celibacy of the Priest,* Newman, Westminster, 1963, pp. 20, 21.

[7] *Ibid.*

[8] Quoted in R. V. Sampson, *The Psychology of Power,* Pantheon Books, New York, 1966, p. 4.

[9] Cf. Tom Driver, "Sexuality and Jesus," *New Theology,* Vol. 3, ed. by Martin E. Marty and D. G. Peerman, Macmillan, New York, 1966, pp. 118-133.

[10] Cf. Eugene C. Kennedy, M.M., *Fashion Me a People: Man, Woman, and the Church,* Sheed & Ward, New York, 1967.

[11] Cf. David Burrell, C.S.C., "The Other Side of the Celibacy Question," *National Catholic Reporter,* September 6, 1967.

[12] Cf. David P. O'Neill, *Priestly Celibacy and Maturity,* Sheed & Ward, New York, 1965.

III

Sexual Development—The Individual and the Community

III

IF SEXUALITY is to become demythologized and yet remain human and important, new attitudes to sexual morality must take the place of fearful adherence to unquestioned rules of sexual conduct. Legalistic strictures and rigid obedience cannot accompany a realization that human sexuality is part of human expressiveness, a way to grow in self-knowledge and self-giving and communication with others. A morality aimed at growth in human sexuality must replace a tidy sexual calculus. But just how do we grow to personal integrity and generativity (to use Eriksonian language again)? How do we learn to love God and our neighbor as our self through our human sexuality?

In the ideal situation of human sexuality, as affirmed in the first chapters, each person could freely express committed love for other persons with joy, pleasure, and playful sexual expressiveness. Just as in marriage the playful freedom of pregenitality can merge with and enhance the violent necessity of sexual ecstasy, so in the ideal human state diverse loves for one and many could be freely expressed and received without conflict. All the creative joys and delights of sexual community and expression should be a part of human fulfillment. Inhibition and limitation have no value in themselves. Man, who in intellect is distinguished by his ability to conceive infinity, is distinguished in emotion by his ability to have limitless desire. As Freud and others have shown, man never gives up anything in the land of his desires if he can help it. Why, after all, should he?

In the Christian view, pleasure, play, joy, and love are all part of the creation; and they are all good. Sacrifice and limitations are just that, unfortunate necessities to sorrow over. All of the limitations and sufferings of Christ's followers and fellows grieved him. Suffering, sacrifice, grief, and discontent are meaningless without the restitution and triumph of the resurrection. Just as Job received back family and riches after his ordeal (and this strikes moderns as crass) so Christians are told to run a good race since God prepares for them "what no eye has ever seen or ear heard." Sacrifice, hardship, self-limitation, only have value "for the sake of the kingdom"; crosses are taken up only to follow Christ in service and love for others. Inhibition or the blocking of desire and action must be aimed at some higher good, some greater growth, some fuller life. At the same time, however, an orthodox Christian view of reality clearly accepts the fact that in this world, before the final triumph, the remaining existence of sin and evil will necessitate inhibition of desires. Human limitations will be overcome by self-limitations, not by a totally free behavior which selfishly ignores the bondage of the human condition, of the whole creation "groaning for redemption."

Why speak of human bondage? Because there seem to be two aspects of reality which produce and provoke constraint: the fact that man cannot survive in a sometimes hostile world without other men, and the fact that man grows and develops in time and space and finally dies. Man depends upon other men not only for material necessities, but also because human survival depends upon culture conveyed through human communication. But life together means life restrained. The good of the group and the good of the individual are often in conflict. Individual desires of possessiveness, aggression, sexual fulfillment, even of speech and work, clash with the same desires in other individuals. Time and space impose obvious limits; the same territory, the same mate, the same tools, etc., cannot be at the disposal of more than one individual at a time. Animal species solve the problems of aggression, mating, and group survival with built-in instincts of inhibition and limited times and territories for sexual desire and activity. Man, who desires all the time and knows it, must create and impose limitations through cultural means. The desire for love from others and the ability to love the self and approve of the self become dependent upon membership in a group and upon one's contribution to the group's well-being. Approval by "significant others" becomes as important a pleasure as one's own desires; human socialization is a complex cultural process.

Another result of living in continuing time and limited space is the impossibility of instantaneous development. Man grows through stages of development, with each new stage built upon his previous capacities. Because of this process, however, the limitations of the growing organism impose a turning away from a present satisfaction to obtain a future fuller satisfaction. This innate human drive to grow, to desire more, to overcome limits, to use more and more human potential, is rather awesome to consider. The baby striving to explore the world and master the difficult feat of walking keeps trying despite the pain of falls. He rejects the easy alternative of staying with the mastered art of crawling. Children struggle to speak, giving up private sounds in order to join the human community of commonly understood language. Unfortunately, each of these stages or graduations requires individual and social negation of other immediately satisfying practices. Frustration, discontent, negation, and dissatisfaction, whether innate or socially induced, spur human development. Human beings who can symbolize, conceive future possibilities, and are self-consciously aware of their own future death can also freely choose self-inhibition for future satisfactions and communal concerns. Man alone of all the species can make promises; he can choose to shape his future, and shape it cooperatively.

Through foresight and group cooperation, communities of men have been able to adapt spectacularly to their environment. The human young can thus get the extended care that they need; the old can be cared for and buried; the young can be initiated into the group to produce and procreate in their turn. Material and symbolic human culture gives substitute pleasures for unrestrained individual fulfillment. When each individual can participate in the benefits of the overall communal life, then the pleasures of living in community outweigh the necessary individual restraints. In fact, as seen in the Christian view of man (and as already discussed in detail in the previous chapter), man can sublimate and substitute satisfactions in order to become primarily a communal man.

Yet beyond the social communal need for order and restraint is a need that arises from some disorder within man. Whether or not the traditional name of original sin or concupiscence is given to the difficulty, the human situation remains the same: man is divided and cannot freely do as he would do. St. Paul aptly expressed a universal reaction to life when he said, "Though the will to do what is good is in me, the performance is not . . . instead of doing the good things I want to do, I carry out the sinful things I do not want."[1] In the new theological interpretations of man's concupiscence, this lack of inner freedom and tendency to sluggish inertia is well analyzed. Karl Rahner has tellingly shown that this lack of wholeness and free self-direction even keeps man from committing evil acts freely.[2] This theological analysis of man's divided condition not only fits the common experience of man, but it may find corroboration in another realm of discourse. When psychologists speak of "resistances," "obsessions," "compulsions," a "death-wish," all of which resist change and growth, it sounds suspiciously like theological discussions of concupiscence. Something within man keeps him from constantly and instantly doing what he thinks he should, even from doing what he deeply desires to do. Any moral or social analysis which does not recognize man's inner disabilities and lack of wholeness is doomed to failure. Many a utopian community has foundered under the assumption that man's perfection was innate and could be assured solely by living in a corrected social system. Unfortunately, the "built-in" problems of the individual's inner development remain.

Orthodox Christian tradition, however, has erred in the opposite direction by ignoring or minimizing social influence and concentrating instead on the isolated individual and, in particular, on his sexuality as the focus of sin. Human sexuality was all but equated with original sin, concupiscence with sexual desire. St. Paul's use of the word "flesh" was narrowly interpreted as man's physical nature in general and his sexual desires in particular. Now, of course, biblical scholars agree that St. Paul's use of "flesh" included all the faculties of man that resist the Spirit; mental and "spiritual" faculties can be as divisive and rebellious against love of others as sexual desire or physical indulgence. Yet, because of the dismal gnostic influences cataloged in the previous chapters, for generations of Christians "the flesh" meant sexuality, and "morality" meant sexual morality. Sex, feared and overestimated, became isolated from the totality of human life and human development. Sexual sins were the very worst kind of offenses ("all sexual sins are mortal"). Sexual virtue was the supreme virtue. Chastity for the sake of chastity rather than charity became more important than social justice, verbal charity, or active good works. Puritanical western cultures became obsessed with avoiding sexual sin, outlawing one pleasure after another in order to escape being led down the path to perdition.

No past era surpassed the nineteenth century in its zenith of cultural suppression of sexuality. Everything physical became unmentionable; and ridiculous extremes resulted, such as religious teachers and their secular counterparts instructing the young to bathe in their underwear for modesty's sake. The uproarious examples of sexual denial and prudery are almost unbelievable today, except for the fact that so many adults retain the scars of their sexual miseducation. Of course, a sexual reaction and sexual revolution had to come. Unfortunately, however, in the effort to overthrow the prevalent suspicions, suppressions, and pessimism, sexuality became glorified, glamorized, and exempt from all moral categories. It remained isolated, specialized, romantically asocial, an individual and personal matter only: private sexual behavior became sacrosanct.

Such rampant sexual individualism is no more tenable than any other self-centered disregard for the community. A laissez-faire sexual morality is as harmful as a laissez-faire business ethic. Man is a communal social species, and the good of each individual is unalterably intertwined with the good of all. If, for instance, lying and disregard for truth are widespread within a community, not only does each individual run the risk of losing the ability to distinguish fact from illusion but mutual trust and efficient cooperation also break down. The use of language affects a group's adaptation to the environment and the challenges of reality. Words conveying only illusions mislead and confuse group efforts to cope with reality. In a more private realm, the misuse of language within a family can seriously disturb human development. If the verbal message is different from the nonverbal message, the confusion can be destructive. All of man's important media of expression affect both the private and the social good; and sexual development and expressiveness is as individually and communally important as man's words, work, property, and money.

A demythologized sexual morality must foster an individual love of self which will lead to a love of neighbor, with full recognition of the reality of man's communal and social situation. *The* great communal dimension of sexuality is, of course, procreation—upon which the continuance of the community in time depends. Even if or when babies are actually grown in glass wombs from stored sperm and ova, procreative potential will remain all-important for the species. Man is man because he remembers the past, knows the present is temporary, and can project into the future. Any ideal or ethic which treats of man's present individual sexual behavior (or any other behavior) without consideration of men's past, future, and social situation does not present a fully human ideal. As long as men die, other men intent upon survival cannot ignore the interdependence of man, the future, or procreation. A recognition that the present generation will pass away provokes concern for the community and for future generations. It is not surprising that our current western denial of death (for many, the only taboo remaining in society) accompanies a rampant individualism and present-oriented pragmatism.

Any valid ideal of sexual behavior, then, must include the expansiveness of past and future social consciousness. On the other hand, behavior should not be so chained to the group past or so immersed in a communal future that the present and the individual are given no rights or consideration. Nor should the individual's present be sacrificed to an individualistic future, as in the grotesque Horatio Alger ethics of success, achievement, and individual rewards in the future. Total suppression of all present individual pleasure is dehumanizing. Sexual pleasure can be sublimated into the expansive pleasures of friendship, procreation, contemplation, art, work, play; but to attempt total deprivation of pleasure for any reason is to attempt to turn man into either an animal or a machine. Love, joy, pleasure, and personal participation in community are also unique attributes of man made in the image of God. A sexual ethic which revolts at pleasure for pleasure's sake has not accepted the nature of man or the universe. At the same time, an ethic which cannot understand the exchange of present individual pleasures for communal and future joys is equally distorted. A truly balanced and wise culture would be able to hold values which incorporated pleasures individual and communal, immediate and sublimated, with an intense consciousness of the present always balanced by respect for the past and concern for the future.

Christians have not yet been able to achieve such a fully balanced synthesis. The doctrines of creation and incarnation emphasize man's past and history; the belief in the parousia, the second coming, and heaven emphasize man's future; while consciousness of the risen Christ's presence and the Holy Spirit's power focus attention on the present moment. Whenever some of these doctrines are ignored while others are overemphasized, a most distorted Christian culture appears.

One of the most damaging distortions in western Christianity was the withering of consciousness of the Holy Spirit and a theology of the resurrection. Theological concern and devotion focused on the cross or on heaven, on either past or future. Christians did not emphasize the Spirit working in the present within individuals, urging them individually and collectively to new growth and understanding. The presence of the resurrected Christ was also ignored; without consciousness or affirmation of the resurrection of the body, the human bodies present in this world were devalued. Living human bodies could be tortured and burned for the good of their future souls if the person did not adhere to rigid objective formulations of past revelations. Claims that the Spirit was inspiring change, growth, and love were suspect. Morality and an ethic of behavior became external and over-objective, while a positive sense of community and of the dignity of the individual Christian empowered and growing in the Spirit were devalued. Naturally, when heretical sects arose to challenge the legalistic western Church, they invariably over-stressed present freedom in the Spirit, again separating the self from the body's past and future. An ethic that denies past and future confines the human ideal, whether that ethic be a religious or secular one.

Another terrible distortion which past Christian societies have shared with other cultures included forced compliance with the community's standards. Lack of personal freedom has been effected by group penalties ranging from verbal shaming to lynching. Ostracism, imprisonment, and economic reprisals have all been used as forms of societal pressure to enforce codes and rules. Some cultures have attempted to use laws to insure not only public but private conformity. Yet the use of any force seems to belie Christian ideals. Clearly, persuasion and example were Christ's methods to draw men to him. Christ enjoined love, teaching, and peaceful means on his followers. He criticized his followers who were concerned with punishing and exacting revenge upon those who did not respond or actively opposed him. Except for a certain amount of indignation and denunciation of false religious teachers, Christ emphasized mercy for the sinner and restraint in moral judgment. Love for enemies, reconciliation, forgiveness—these were the marks of the new and better Christian way. Christians must not return evil for evil, but must overcome evil with good.

The Christian ideal is certainly psychologically sound. To concentrate on evil and sin can be a way of admitting evil into the personality without recognition of active responsibility. Those who compulsively search out sin are as enslaved as the sinner. Worse still, in a communal context, the search for and punishment of sinners creates such an atmosphere of suspicion and fear that individuals can be driven to the expected behavior. A classic case in European history is the agony of the witch-hunts. The more witches were feared, the more they were searched out, the greater and more widespread were the delusions on the part of both victims and persecutors. Modern parallels come immediately to mind: red scares, riots, purges, and panics, all destructive and harmful to individuals and society. Fear and expectation of evil, along with desire for revenge on those who break the standard, corrupt individual growth in love for others. Private morality is all-important to the common good, but a high level of virtue cannot be obtained by coercion and law. Extensive social pressure and punitive emotions and measures destroy the freedom to choose, the unique characteristic of man.

A wise community would keep the actual enforcement of communal standards to a minimum. Perhaps only that behavior which immediately and aggressively harms another should be socially restrained. The movement to repeal laws punishing private sexual activities between consenting adults serves the important freedom of the individual to choose, and moves away from a prosecuting process of society which degrades rather than protects the group morality. The repellent and horrible irony in every "crusade" for morality is that instead of imitating the sacrificial love of the cross, specifically chosen by Christ instead of force, the crusaders zealously use force without concern for their own means. In detecting private sexual crimes, for example, officers have practiced enticement, invasion of privacy, and even coercion in obtaining confessions. "Crusades" using force to effect standards are a sure sign of failure, whether the issue be sexuality, religion, or patriotism, whether the arena be family, church, or state.

However, while remaining committed to the minimal use of force, the community must also care about and voice commitment to standards, as well as live them. In small tribal groups, the intimacy of life together may subtly convey the standards to all (as was also done in certain aristocratic elites). In a more complex pluralistic society with conflicting and confusing values, it becomes necessary for individual subgroups to state convictions and work for clarification of standards and commitments.[3] The community cannot be ignored in a complete retreat to private morality. Psychologists have consistently noticed the confusion of children and youth when they can find no adult firmness of principles. The function of being an adult who assumes generative concern for the rest of the community and for future generations includes an expression of the adult operating values which the next generation can apprehend and test itself against. How can young people grow up confronting a vacuum—nothing to accept, or rebel against, or improve upon?

Christians in the western community, therefore, have a twofold mission: to assert a clear persuasive ideal of communal behavior and to keep communal coercion of group standards to a minimum. Energy, time, effort, and money spent on policing and coercing is taken away from efforts to educate and facilitate human development. To concentrate on man's inner lack of freedom and wholeness, to treat men as hopeless sinners inclined to evil, crush human capacity for hope and growth. One of the most illuminating biblical texts describing God's servant should be remembered in every discussion of morality: "He does not break the crushed reed, nor quench the wavering flame."[4] Surely it is possible to create a society in which communal values can be combined with mercy for those who do not meet them. Tolerance need not be the fruit of indifference. Cannot a secure high civilization embody high ideals with a minimum of coercion? The concepts of human freedom to choose and the perpetual growth open to each human being inspire a far better culture than enforced external conformity.

When, however, the reality of human life presents necessary and inevitable limitations which cannot now be overcome, man gains nothing by denial of the limits. The creative human solution is, rather, to take the limitation and use it to stimulate growth and personality development and communal well-being. Faced with a biological imperative or an environmental limitation, man must not only adapt but can elaborate and improve. This pattern has been exemplified over and over again in man's history: food is turned into cuisine, shelter into architecture, clothing into fashion, communication into language, mating into marriage, procreation into family life, group survival into community. Even man's bondage and his inner divisions producing evil actions have intensified the quest for inner goodness, justice, and understanding. The most ancient Egyptian papyri wrestle with the problem of the existence of evil. Man, realizing the limitations of life, is able to creatively use and overcome them, growing at the same time through other denials and necessary sacrifices.

Necessary denial of sexual expression, therefore, should creatively be used to further an integrated human self with a capacity for sexual self-expression that is not isolated from the whole personality. The ideal of a whole, undivided man expressing himself authentically in all of his thoughts and behavior has persisted throughout diverse cultures. Erik Erikson claims that every human life cycle aims at integrity and that men of integrity in any culture or civilization will have an affinity and similarity with other integrated personalities. This may be. Certainly, high civilizations have revered the self-collected man of truth whose word and deeds are one in seeking the good. A socially defined consensus of required inner coherence, order, and stability differentiates the mentally well from the psychotic, who is inwardly divided and confused. Since sex is one of the important ways man knows himself and communicates with others, it is extremely important that in his sexuality he does not contradict himself or misrepresent himself to others. Ideally, expressions of sexuality should be integrated with all the rest of an individual's life, his emotions, his reasoning, his work, his words, his community relations. Each nonintegrated sexual act or expression contributes to the divisions that man tries to overcome and heal within himself and in his relations with others.

Since man is variable and developing within time, however, his sexuality will be expressing a different self-consciousness and different communications with others at different times. What is appropriate at one time is not at another. Once the limits of reality have been granted, then one of the human tasks of growth is to express or inhibit behavior appropriately. Just as a person comes to an understanding of when and what to say to whom, so appropriate sexual behavior is learned. Control of the tongue in the service of love of self, of God and others, is usually far more difficult than the appropriate living of sexuality (as St. James so well understood). But since Christ's teaching on the use of language was more or less ignored while the Christian emphasis upon sexual sin mushroomed, moderns are conditioned to a sexual conscience without a corresponding concern for the morality of speech—or, for that matter, of money, property, or work. It can well bear repeating that a restored Christian ethic will de-emphasize individualistic and isolated sins, especially in the area of sexuality, and will instead emphasize the person's total behavior in all the different areas of his personal and communal life.

However, even in such an ethic, with a goal of integrated love, some sexual behavior will be seen as hurting the self and others, as a refusal to grow, as a choice of bondage. Unfortunately, man has erroneously denied his sexual humanity or human sexuality in many various ways throughout his history. Some men have turned away from man in forms of bestiality; some have dehumanized man by fusing sexuality with aggression or with economic exchange. Clearly, bestiality repudiates the self-identity of man and his self-acceptance as a member of the unique human community: man tries to evade himself by using a subhuman object for his own sexual pleasure. This denies sexuality any human reciprocity, mutuality, or procreative purpose. The Olympians of Greek myth often raped humanity in the guise of animals, an interesting revelation of primitive man's dependence-fear, attraction-repulsion relationship with animals. Animals were seen as potent functionaries in the sacral universe, even as divine in primitive religions. The early Hebrews were forbidden bestiality partly as a protest against pagan religious rites. Israel and Christianity affirmed man's position as uniquely created in the image of God, who freely created the universe and gave man dominion over the animals. And, of course, in an urbanized civilized world like our own, manifestations of bestiality are seen as signs of severe mental and emotional disturbance, a malfunctioning of growth toward the human.

Human sensitivity to male sexual aggression toward

women has also grown. If mating by capture was ever culturally approved, it was so only by denying women full personhood. To deny free sexual consent denies the humanity of the other person. The use of force in any sexual relationship is dehumanizing; and the more harmful to another, the more dehumanizing and the more horrible. Damage to the growth of the aggressor's own personality is also disastrous. A person who fuses aggression and the sexual drive suffers a major distortion of human development; learning to love a whole person as a whole person becomes hopeless.

Buying or selling sexual expression similarly degrades the human person. In prostitution, sexuality is detached from the rest of the personality. The giving and receiving expresses no more than an economic transaction. Since the relationship would not exist without the economic inducement, it cannot be free or truly mutual. Actions which could be expressing love, commitment, even free play and pleasure, are reduced to the confining narrowness of economic considerations, not to mention inner contradictions. Sexuality cannot be a fully human expression when the sexual object is subhuman, or another person submitting to aggressive or economic pressure.

Apart from the dehumanizing distortions just discussed, much of the anxiety and difficulty in growing up into sexual integrity and wholeness comes from the three great denials necessary to develop an ideal of adult heterosexual genitality. Western Judeo-Christian culture has insisted that each individual give up incest, masturbation, and homosexual relationships. These prohibitions or taboos have been sanctioned by revelation, social structure, and natural law reasoning. When the authority of revelation and natural law diminished among modern secular men, the needs of society remained. Moreover, these external social necessities were supported by most psychoanalytic theory in its claim that the inner psychosexual development of man requires giving up immediate immature stages of development for complete maturity, defined as the potential for a heterosexual genital relationship.

As psychoanalytic theory validated the traditional sexual insistence on heterosexual genitality, it explained the path man takes to psychosexual maturity. Each so-called perversion was seen as corresponding to a sexual developmental stage among men. Horror at man's unnatural perversions and vicious behavior could finally give way to knowledge. Human pride may have been hurt by the newly revealed human similarity between saint and sinner, but the new insights into personality helped to create a positive atmosphere encouraging growth rather than an anxious, punitive, static approach wherein people "fall into sin" and "are lost." The knowledge that all human beings are operating in a continuum of development gives hope to the immature in difficulties, and modesty and mercifulness to the successful. Every person has had to forego the most fundamental desires and overcome them for his own growth and the good of society. The limitations of the human situation spare no one.

Incest is a necessary primal taboo of human sexuality, all-important in its social implication, for the integrity and effectiveness of individuals and human social groups depend upon the results of the prolonged child-rearing period humans require. Not only does the prohibition of incest promote genetic variety and strength, but it also maintains family discipline, family unity, and general social cohesion. Parents must have a strong bond between them to present a united front and work together to protect and rear their children. Additional sexual dependency, attractions, and jealousy would over-complicate and strain intrafamily relationships, destroying mutual cooperation. Extra-family marriages provide genetic and social stimulation in the larger society with the mutual benefits of kinship ties.

On the more subtle personal level, incest stunts the psychic growth of personality. Parent-child relationships which would fulfill the natural desires of infants for physical and psychic unity would also keep children infantile, insulated from peers and community. Sibling sexual relationships would close individuals to the influences of parents and culture. Personality grows from a frustrated turning away from the family to contact with unfamiliar relationships and the extra-family environment. Those who cannot accept the primal limitation remain within the womb of the family and never grow up. A computer may match twin brother and sister as perfect mates (as happened in one recent computer session), but the common human wisdom in almost every society has known that man must leave father, mother, sister, brother, and form a new one-flesh unity.

Cultures provide appropriate incest taboos according to the group's living conditions. Primitive groups, living communally, marrying young, with much dependence upon extended families and strong kinship ties, need stringent avoidance techniques and sanctions. Men and women may speak different languages, and a man may not be permitted to speak to his mother-in-law or his sister. In one known case (proving the strength of these inhibitions), Ishi, the last male Indian of a small tribe in the California hills, supported until their deaths an older woman and a young female cousin, both of a tabooed kinship, without any sexual relationship. His tribe perished, but he maintained his stone-age culture with dignity until the end. The anthropologists who knew and worked with him also reported him free of masturbation despite his hard and lonely life.

The problem of masturbation as another painful primal denial may appear most commonly in complicated, insecure, or psychically hostile cultures. With no sure cultural self-definition or energy-absorbing work or play, without early marriage or communal ties, a person feels sexual tension to be overwhelming and satisfies himself with himself. Perhaps, too, at particular stages of development involving exploration of the self, masturbation may be as inevitable as a baby's thumbsucking. Surrounded by uncertainty, one resorts to one's own body as secure and dependable; some intense pleasure and comfort can be had in a hard, hostile, and difficult life—"I confirm myself to myself." But just as thumbsucking impedes speech and manual dexterity, so the pleasure and the accompanying fantasy of masturbation cannot be directed to activity or generativity.

There are some theories that masturbatory fantasies are disguised incestuous wishes, which, if true, would explain the anxiety and guilt even when children have never been threatened or punished. Also, dependent and compulsively frequent reliance on any present immediate passive satisfaction can characterize neurotic behavior. In its retreat to self and fantasy, masturbation can inhibit development. However, much more danger to human development has probably been created by the castigation of "self-abuse." Such overreaction expressed much manichaean and ascetic hatred of the flesh. To equate masturbation with a mortal sin such as murder is ridiculous. The resulting cruelty to toddlers and adolescents reminds one of the nannies who devised mechanical vises to control the "vile" and "nasty" thumbsucking of children. Cultural energy can better be directed to supporting youth's strong motivations to grow out of self-centered exploration and the desire for immediate comfort (so naturally prevalent during adolescence) toward new and real mutual relationships and less mechanical pleasures.

Masturbation throughout life (despite its recommendation by some sexologists) may lead to a diminished ability to give and receive pleasure in the married sexual relationship. The mechanics of one, two, three, release, does not develop reciprocal sensitivity to mutual play and pleasure. Moreover, the personality strength gained through successful suppression of private, unsocial sexual pleasure and fantasy works toward that wholeness of personality which is necessary to attend to another, to truly give to another a whole self.

It is just this inability to give a whole self, with all one's potential, which makes a homosexual relationship incomplete. The secular disciplines remain divided, whether homosexuality is a symptom or a way of life. Most psychiatrists, and those adhering to the Freudian model of human development, see homosexual inclination and practice as symptomatic of immaturity and lack of psychosexual growth. Through some malfunctioning, the person never achieves a secure identification with his or her own sexual identity or the ability to relate in a mature genital relationship with the opposite sex. When the potential and capacity for heterosexual genitality is not achieved, goes this theory, neither is a mature personality. The unstable, neurotic nature of most homosexual alliances is then adduced as proof of faulty personalities. But, say some homosexuals in reply (backed by a few experts), it is persecution and rejection by the heterosexual society that produces the neurotic "gay society." These homosexuals claim that there would be more mature homosexuals and more stable relationships between them if the general society would become more permissive in their regard.

Assuming briefly that active homosexuality is a free choice based on inner predisposition rather than a symptom, can it be an acceptable choice? To choose a specifically sexual intimacy as the expression of love for someone of one's own sex necessitates many major rejections and denials. Not only is the past evolutionary process of heterosexual human development rejected generally, but, more specifically, the immediate past parental procreative process is denied. The homosexual reacts against the relationship of his or her parents which produced his own existence. More damaging still, the rejection of the past procreative reality accompanies the impossibility of future personal procreativity. No children, no responsibility of child-bearing, can intrude upon the couple's relationship; the relationship can only remain closed. Homosexuals are caught in an exclusive, self-centered love confining pleasure to an isolated present which cannot include affirmation of the past or the future, or their own present reproductive structures of sexuality. Such radical denial of the person's past, present, and potential divides man and negates community. A desire to give one's self to the other sex is a first step in healing divisions and in reaching the larger community of man. However natural, normal, or understandable homosexual love may be as a process of human development,[5] it can only be unsatisfactory to stay in this stage, growing no more. Can one become mature, loving, and responsible amidst so many crucial rejections of self, the opposite sex, and the human community? It seems apparent, too, that the homosexual couple would succumb even more easily than the heterosexual couple to an exclusive romantic couple mystique.

Societies which encourage or accept homosexuality as a norm become enmeshed in rejections. The Greeks, for instance, denied education and civil freedoms to women, who were also deprived of rights and authority even in the home. Women were not expected to develop personalities which could provide intellectual and cultural companionship to men. Love, procreation, and friendship could not be united in the male-female relationship. Furthermore, the Greek civilization and communities were scarred by infanticide and by nonacceptance of manual laborers, slaves, and foreigners as full persons. It would be interesting to study further those cultures which have accepted homosexual ideals and, in particular, to study possible relationships between acceptance of such ideals and "generative" concern for new life and the future of the community. Basically, homosexuality is not viciously unnatural or monstrous. It is only more subject to a selfish exclusiveness regarding community.

In homosexuality, as in masturbation, the panic and horror of condemnation becomes another serious difficulty for the person to overcome. A temporary episode in development does not determine a whole life. If society punishes, despises, and scorns homosexuality, then the person is more easily trapped into fear and desperation. Where a nonfearful morality and ethic of growth can prevail, the person can better allay anxiety and hope for a more complete future.[6] Fear of the opposite sex, which many psychiatrists claim underlies much of the homosexual's rejection, may arise from our culture's overemphasis on the polarity of male and female rather than their similarity as human beings. When a very specialized male or female model—rather than the fully developed human personality—prevails in a society, then those persons who do not fit or cannot abide the stereotype will have sexual difficulties. In a society which puts sex in its proper place, important, but not all-important, human sexual growth will be more easily accomplished. Then, as McLuhan and Leonard predict in "The Future of Sex," homosexuality will decline.[7] Certainly, those who cannot or will not live the communal ideal should not be persecuted. Here too, cultural energy could be much better directed in giving them help and understanding and in building up a healthy society which encourages mature heterosexual development within a complete ideal of full personal humanity.

Even when mature heterosexual development and readiness for marriage are achieved, a final difficulty arises in our complicated world. Modern man is biologically ready for mating before he is intellectually mature or educated enough to take a place in the economy. The question of premarital sexual behavior becomes more and more prominent as the biologically mature but premarital stage of life is increasingly extended. Yet, since the time in question is still relatively short in one's life-span, most of which will normally be spent in the married state, premarital sexual behavior may be the least important of all sexual behavior.

In actuality, the choice of a future marriage partner is the crucial problem. What comes before in childhood and what will come afterward in marriage give youthful sexuality its importance. But can the current hue and cry of public bewailers of the "sexual immorality of youth" really be taken seriously? It seems more likely that the old use the young, and especially the student, "as scapegoat."[8] Since youth is a time to explore, experiment, and make mistakes to better prepare for adulthood, the real questions revolve around what behavior best prepares for marriage and what mistakes may impede human growth and development. To these there are really no sure and certain answers.

Easy analogies between our present western society and more primitive societies which sanction either rigid abstinence or free premarital affairs break down because our own society is much more complex and each individual must play more complicated roles. The adolescent sexual freedom of a society like Margaret Mead's Samoa, for instance, cannot be automatically applied. In such a system almost everyone becomes adept at giving and getting sexual pleasure and there is less aggression and tension, but then there is also little achievement, individuality, or orientation to an intense marital attachment. The communal family which keeps incidents of premarital pregnancy from being a disaster also engulfs the individual, the marital pair, and the parent-child relationship. A lack of sexual inhibition and restraint in adolescence can be easily managed in a culture in which survival does not depend upon individual disciplined effort to achieve and learn.

In our complex western culture, however, self-discipline, or the ability to give up a present satisfaction for a future fulfillment, is an absolute necessity. Not only does education take many years and much individual effort, but a more differentiated personality is needed to withstand everyday conflicts and psychological pressures. Sexual restraint, self-mastery, sublimation, and self-control are integral to our culture, which requires a strong sense of individuality and selfhood to overcome obstacles and control emotional impulses. If the electronic era of the future creates a new tribalism, perhaps western culture will change completely. At this point, however, a strong individualism based on long-range goals is important.

Furthermore, an increased intensity in a reciprocal marriage relationship can only be built upon the greater self-identity which grows from a highly developed concept of fidelity and loyalty. "Fidelity" as defined by Erik Erikson is that particular virtue developed in adolescence "to sustain loyalties freely pledged in spite of the inevitable contradiction of value ssytems." Erikson therefore questions whether "early freedom in the direct use of his sexuality would make man freer as a person?"[9] In the past, only female chastity mattered, combining a "damaged goods" concept, with a concern to keep the inheritance lines intact. Thankfully, female emancipation promotes women's development as people and encourages more idealistic attitudes toward sexual norms. Personal growth through active choice can only emerge with the passing of legalisms and the end of puritanical purity motifs of physical and moral contamination. Intercourse, of itself neither soils nor perfects the person, nor is it an indifferent act. In a Christian and humanistic ethic, sexual acts, like all important human acts, should express a person's emotions, will, and rationality simultaneously. When a regard for integrated actions joins with an adherence to marital commitment and fidelity to one's future, then premarital chastity can be freely chosen by both men and women. Sex is a basic expression of the self; and, ideally, complete genital union with another should express a correspondingly complete rational and emotional union of work, play, and commitment.

Not only should the sexual relationship express the freedom and integrity of private aspects of a couple's personal unity, but the private relationship of the couple should not have to be contradicted in their social public life. Discontinuity between private and public action too easily becomes a form of lying and self-deceit. Significantly, Kinsey's statistics showed more marital infidelity among those who had had premarital sexual experience. One of the basic ways we come to know ourselves is by our actions, and the reluctance to establish a full or lasting community of life and work in marriage casts doubts on the integrity of love and the maturity of lovers. Mature persons open to the future and willing to accept responsibility for the care of others accept the continuity of promises and institutions as an enrichment of love. What does love mean if it refuses concern and commitment beyond the present moment or isolates itself from all other expressions of man but the sexual expression? Engaged couples, of course, have already committed themselves socially and entered into a community of life. If permanent commitment to each other has been made and meant, then sexual intercourse transforms their betrothal into clandestine marriage, a different moral situation. Clandestine marriage, however, confuses the social order and makes any marriage rite anticlimactic. Verbal commitment, sexual commitment, and social commitment given together mutually help keep the inner and outer man from divisions and build up the human community.

A human ideal or ethic or moral sexual behavior begins and ends with the fact that humans living in community face the sad necessity of overcoming human and environmental limitations by selective self-limitations. The human challenge is to choose only those limitations which will provoke human growth and more complex satisfactions. Unnecessary irrational taboos beyond the repressions necessary to communal life burden mankind and retard growth. On the other hand, a boundless faith in complete human freedom of all sexual impulses is also disastrous for the human community.

At this time in history, western society struggles with a sexual revolution just as Christianity wrestles with reappraisals and renewal. Hopefully, the Christian vision of the possibilities of human development can contribute to, if not dominate, the whole human community's quest for a human ethic. Christians who, in their human sexuality as in everything else, are committed to the light yoke of Christ which produces joy and liberty in hope are challenged to live this anew in order to convey to others the meaning of their ideal. Painful efforts to grow up human, rather than absurd, must produce concrete results. Why should the young keep trying if adult life will only be sterile and hollow? With censoriousness, prudery, and pride removed from the traditional Christian ethic, it can more effectively serve as the "leaven" in society. This "leaven" could encourage understanding and help in, rather than overreaction to, sexual lapses, "illegimate" birth, so-called "perversions." While love for the whole man would see beyond social stigma, Christians can and must remain committed to the perfection of man and continue to aspire to and hold the highest ideals of love and sexual behavior.

NOTES

[1] Rom. 7:18-19.

[2] Cf. Karl Rahner, S.J., *Theological Investigations,* Vol. I, Helicon, Baltimore, 1961, p. 366.

[3] Cf. The Group for the Advancement of Psychiatry, Committee on the College Student, *Sex and the College Student,* Atheneum, New York, 1965.

[4] Is. 42:3.

[5] Cf. John Harvey, O.S.F.S., "Morality and Pastoral Treatment of Homosexuality," *Continuum,* Summer 1967, Vol. V, No. 2, pp. 279-297. The excellence of this fine article pleading for love and understanding is unfortunately marred by a certain degree of antisexual prejudice—which, for example, resulted in the statement that a homosexual relationship "begun as an apparent resurrection of the spirit *deteriorates* into a resurrection of the flesh" (p. 283) .

[6] Cf. Helmut Thielicke, *The Ethics of Sex,* Harper, New York, 1964, pp. 269-287.

[7] Cf. Marshall McLuhan and George Leonard, "The Future of Sex," *Look,* July 25, 1967.

[8] Cf. Richard F. Hettlinger, *Living with Sex: The Student's Dilemma,* Seabury, New York, 1966, p. 16.

[9] Erik Erikson, *Insight and Responsibility,* Norton, New York, 1964, pp. 124-125.

IV

Sexuality in Marriage: Mutuality and Freedom

UNBALANCED VIEWS of sexuality have contributed to much distortion in writings about marriage. Theology and marriage manuals have sometimes gone as far astray as the vast body of popular "wisdom" parlayed in the press. Many have misled and been misled; innumerable marriages have suffered. The errors and excesses, some of which have already been touched on in the previous chapters, center around two opposite poles or attitudes, both of which view human sexuality from too limited a viewpoint.

One limiting attitude toward married sexuality might be called the reductionist approach. Whether the reductionism is theological or biological, technical analysis reigns. Theologically, this analysis has taken up questions of the definition of the marriage act, of the rights, duties, and uses of sexuality in marriage. Since these discussions originated historically amidst disputes over marriage involving clashing individuals and clashing customs of different groups of newly baptized peoples, the Roman legal approach and attitude remained dominant. Harried Christian theologians had to forge a basic position under the pressure of problems compounded by complicated problems. Since marriage, an omnipresent phenomenon, involved the welfare of couples, parents, children, royal houses, and the general society, solutions and decisions could not wait. Caught up in questions of law and social organization, the thinking on married sexuality was reduced to definitions and proscriptions concerning the physical acts which consummated marriage and produced children. The beginnings of a theology of marriage were swamped by the continual crises of conversions, reformation, counterreformation, revolution, and modernism.[1]

A reductionist, technical preoccupation has also dominated emerging secular approaches to sexuality in marriage. Definitions and descriptions center around terminology and techniques. Scholastic discussions of impediment to acts are replayed, but focused now on erections and orgasms. The emphasis on physical adjustments and criteria is so stressed that much of the secular writing about married sexuality remains mechanical. Ritual references to love and unity and other "psychic factors" seem but a sop thrown to the multitude for reassurance. The important part of sexuality is again measurable achievement, working up a repertoire of successful sexual techniques. Quantification is the basic mode of perception: How many erotogenic zones? How many positions? How many orgasms within how much time? In an ABZ of married love, how far along are you; how many of the 206 possible positions have you worked through?

The natural human reaction against the reductionist views of marriage, both theological and biological, has been to retreat to romanticism. Confronted with legalistic discussions of natural law or extended technical discussions of coitus, human beings fight back. In the resulting counterrevolution, married sexuality becomes mystical, ethereal, and spiritualized. In the name of love, sex is affirmed; but it seems to have little to do with ordinary human male and female bodies. Christians writing about marriage and sex have, in typical monophysite style, let the whole human reality be swallowed up in the divine mystery. Man and wife are supposedly recreating the love of the Trinity, showing forth the Divine Bridegroom's love of the Church, or participating in a creative mystery. Sexuality becomes more mysterious and sacred than anything the pagan temples of Aphrodite could offer. In reaction to the bed as laboratory or to the bed as moral and legal courtroom, the bed must need become altar. Sex blooms as an exercise in encounter, and I-thou experience, with much meditation upon mystery and recitations of the Song of Songs.

This romantic seriousness and high tone cannot be blamed on Christianity alone. It is part of the earnest, high culture that gradually seeped over the west—eclipsing Chaucer, bowdlerizing Shakespeare, elevating everything in its path. Love is the sweet, sad mystery of life; tears are acceptable, but laughter out of place. Togetherness and the romantic union of the couple will give forth the ultimate reality. Male and female polarity and unity produce all creativity (shades of the Yin and Yang, of Father Sky and Mother Earth). Couples will find themselves in each other; couples will know the greatest happiness known to man through love; they will be a world unto themselves. Romantic expectations of marriage have probably never been so high as in our present culture. Marriage books, at least those which are not completely reductionist in view, voice a soaring romanticism. Sometimes, too, quantitative, manipulative mechanics and high-flown, romantic rhetoric alternate in jarring shifts of tone.

One can, however, realize immediately the problems presented to authors. How can any author deal adequately with married sexuality? How is it possible to get everything in, giving the right weight to all the nuances in such complicated, fluctuating realities and relationships? Obviously, it is an impossible task, but a challenging impossibility. At the opposite end of the human spectrum, those chronicling war have somewhat the same problem. There is glory, boredom, humor, heroics, human failure, and the mundane, all confused by the fact that every individual is limited to his own experience. Married sexuality includes the same wide range of individual differences between couples and even between different periods in the couple's life together. In actuality, sexual intercourse is never the same. Punning upon Heraclitus, it might be said that even in marriage one never steps into the same bed. Self, partner, the common relationship—all change. Time passing makes change inevitable.

But this is not to deny certain structural limitations of life: inevitable repetition, continuing identity, material and biological laws. Human change and variety operate within certain finite structures. Man in this life is not infinite, and neither is his sexual experience. There is also an anonymous, limited quality in sexuality which has disturbed moralists as well as those anxiously championing the Infinite Self. The fact that male and female orgasms, at a certain point, follow a patterned sequence of contractions beginning at an 0.8-second frequency, lasting from 6 to 8 contractions, and involving similar tensions and bodily secretions seems to threaten unique self-affirmation. Why must a person follow the common processes of the species? Cannot personal individuality be all-important, all-determining of physical activity? Is not humanity degraded by anonymous biological laws? Is immergence in automatic processes necessarily *submergence*?

The answer to these questions is no. Man need not fear his anonymous animal nature, but must rather accept it. Man can only reach the heights of humanity by going through his anonymous instinctual nature, not by attempting to climb over or around it or to destroy all vestiges of irrationality. The unconscious, anonymous depths of personality are neither automatically bad nor inevitably good. And human judgment, in the experience of centuries, has been able to discern frequent healing powers in the unconscious and irrational. Life itself depends upon the automatic activities of breathing, digestion, and sleep, not to mention the beginning of life in the process of birth. Pleasure, irrationality, and automatic activity are necessary to man. Part of the restorative delight of loving intercourse resides in its incorporation of unconscious depths of personality. Secure selves are not afraid of self-giving in passion, self-abandonment. The individual personality and mutual unity of the couple can be refreshed by participating in one of the fountains of reality, irrational instinct.

Unfortunately, rationalized western man tends to either resist irrationality too much or to go to the other extreme of over-embracing it, often in cults of violence and spontaneity. The delicate balance of thought and emotion is lost to the extremes. "Ripeness is all," said King Lear; but we do not even bloom. We could learn much from other arts and cultures . . . the Zen treatise on the art of archery, the Japanese tea ceremony. Many westerners approach sexuality as swimmers who dive in and then thrash around getting nowhere because they refuse to yield to the element of water and concentrate instead on gasping for air. Panic, flailing uncoordination, tense over-concentration—and the swimmer sinks.

The right use of rationality in married sexual expression calls for a delicate control, the lightest rein. The mature person welcomes desire as a sign of life and love, but spurning the cult of instant gratification submits the desire to reason. If one's mate is away, sick, totally preoccupied in an important matter, reason choses another appropriate expression of love. As silence is to speech, abstinence is to sexual expression. Conscious sublimation can be handled without great emotional turmoil by most happily married couples. And most couples develop an unconscious response to the other's emotional nuances. Sexual sensitivity, tact, and consideration grow naturally; not many need to be told the elementary rules of love. Men and women make the effort to match their mate's mood, to comfort, exult, be serious or merry. Here again, reason gently nudges the emotions and the will.

It is not an offense against romance to plan rationally to arouse and be aroused. Simultaneous desire is the preferred initiative, but, our nature being wounded, man becomes desexualized by work, fatigue, worry over things of this world, by the pace and pattern of modern life in our urban complexes. A couple can sense and judge when they are loosing their focus on each other and their unity, when they are literally "getting out of touch." They then can and should plan privacy, postpone appointments and social obligations, and wait upon their emotions. Sensuality flowers in leisure and relaxation, but America, the land of the stand-up-and-run lunch-counter, has a short supply of leisure. We want to hurry sleep with pills, get drunk quickly, and rush sexual desire. Ultimately, pornography is an abstracted means of hurrying and forcing sexual emotions. Pornography may have its uses, but love and play is far preferable.

With sexual desire present, the mind need discipline itself only to focus on the other person, and to keep that focus and suppress distracting analysis and mental activity. The mystics have given us a full literature of the difficulties and distractions present in cultivating contemplation, but few have admitted or discussed the discipline of attention often necessary to sexual love. Just as the mind flees God, the nonintegrated self evades full sexual focus on another by relapsing into rational thought, irrelevancies, or drifting into self-absorption. The sensual dialectic or dialogue is endangered by mental minutiae, too much or too little activity, too much or too little passivity, and finally too much self-conscious will to succeed. Western man has an inadequate conception of the will; "he has no image of it as passive and receptive, meant as much for rest as for work."[2] Just enough control is needed to keep the fantasy, imagination, and physical activity within the mutual personal sexual realm; too much control kills the freedom of play and desire. Most people battle too much with the demons of a disunified body-mind to achieve simplicity and wholeness in play and passion. A collected, integrated self cannot only give more but can give more easily.

In such an intimate knowing and giving of two people, the secret strengths and divisions of personality will come to light. Laughter heals many of the petty problems of growing whole together, but almost every couple will have some serious sexual failures and conflicts at some point in their marriage. Sexual problems can run the full range of distortions, from a sexual exploitation akin to lust, to a form of sexual accidie or sloth. Whether these conflicts cause bad relationships in other areas of life or are the results of them (in many cases, undoubtedly both), working through these sexual failures strengthens both personal growth and the marriage bond. Sexual communication is interdependent with verbal communication. Each corrects and enriches the other, but openness and true attention to the other is crucial. The present relationship must grow by emphasizing and imagining the future potential rather than remaining trapped in past errors or immaturities. Both persons give up old family romances and illusions in order to concentrate on their own reality and future.

Each couple grows toward unity as they overcome the differences of male and female sexual response which are complicated by their own personalities and sexual histories. What Freud called "the narcissism of small differences" can be outgrown. The usual difference in male and female timing and desires generally necessitates more active wooing, inhibition, and control for the husband. On the other hand, women who may be more complicated sexually as well as being slower in arousal (though capable of multiple orgasms) must cultivate aggressiveness in desire. Sexual generalization, however, is dangerous, because the "usual" male and female differences give way to individual personality differences and cultural conditioning. Age and health are other important factors in differentiating sexuality. It is interesting to note, though, that the Masters and Johnson research on human sexual response concluded that male and female sexuality are more alike than different.[3] Freud's distinction of the feminine response as a more mature vaginal sexuality is now supposedly disproved. Feminine sexual response, like the male orgasm, consists of thrusting contractions of the organism, releasing tension and seeking unity outside itself. The old myths of the woman sexually drawing in the male toward womb and psyche, with inward-directed contractions, remains myth. The feminine contractions in orgasm resemble those of childbirth (appropriately); they are expulsive, and as outer directed as those of the male whose rhythms they match.

Of course, the expectation of sexual fulfillment in orgasms for "good" women is a relatively new cultural phenomenon in the west—new enough so that most women still have to overcome a residue of internalized repression and reserve. This new sexual equality and freedom for women would never have been possible without improved medical care, contraception, and labor-saving devices in the home. Fatigue is a great destroyer of sexual élan, and women who were tired from pregnancies, child-care, and backbreaking labor could not often match the stronger male's insistent sexual drive. There is also some evidence that women mature sexually much later than men, who supposedly reach a peak in their early youth. This difference in the timing of development of sexual energy creates difficulties in mutuality. However, it is impossible to assess how much the general suppression of women also suppressed sexual energy, which is so involved in self-consciousness and self-esteem. Furthermore, feminine fulfillment is also served in the erotic satisfactions of pregnancy, childbirth, nursing, and child-care.

It is not surprising that there are cultures in which female orgasm is completely unknown. Strictly speaking, it is not necesary for the preservation of the species; it may not even be necessary for a happy marriage. Those who have never heard music presumably do not miss it, and people do compensate for missed fulfillments. In a culture such as ours, however, with religious and secular values of unity in marriage and the full development of both partners, the existence of female orgasm cannot be ignored. A high ideal of the individual self and mutuality will naturally include achieving the most intense expression possible: mutual potentiality, with full reciprocal release and relaxation for both man and woman.

The fairly recent extensive publicity and discussion given to feminine orgasm in our culture may already have resulted in overemphasis on achieving this one criterion of sexual success. In the case of female orgasm as "status symbol," anxiety on the part of the man (can he provoke it?) or of the woman (can she produce it?) will be as destructive as any other anxiety or mechanical over-control. Surely, an expression of love can be valid without measuring up to any objective standard. But, of course, with the new idea of mutuality, men must be concerned for the wife's satisfaction; the old concept of total self-absorption of the male in his own pleasure can no longer hold. There is, however, a newly sensitive male in our culture (especially among the under-forty) who matches the newly emancipated woman, and he cannot be fully happy unless his wife shares his sexual joy. These men have integrated sexuality into their personality; not only are they repelled by the detachment of prostitutional sex but also by male detachment or selfishness in marriage. The three out of four college graduates reported by Kinsey as never having been to a prostitute and rarely having been promiscuous do not become husbands, who can disregard their wife's sexuality as their grandfathers did. Among men in the blue-collar classes of America society, too, a much larger number expressed concern with the sexual responsiveness of their wives and held themselves responsible for it."[4]

The new, higher standards for mutuality of fulfillment in sexuality correspond to a new honesty, openness, companionship, and sensitivity in marriage. The old stratagems of women who pretended supreme pleasure to please a husband seem repugnant, a form of deceit. The new standards of marriage and expectations of and for women make retreat from female orgasm as a norm impossible. A culture cannot have it both ways. The "good old days" when women did not "desire" or "care" as much also meant more feminine disdain and coolness to sexuality, more psychic diffidence, and much repressed resentment and hostility toward the husband's "demands." After all, how could any woman half-dead from fatigue not resent being highly stimulated and then left dangling? The remaining physical tension and restlessness is not readily subject to willpower. Love can make sexual frustration tolerable, but it is still a failure in mutuality and a disappointment to sexual desire.

Strong sexual desire is not immoral, but totally human and natural. A strong sense of self and strong desire give an impetus for union with a beloved person. The other's desire is equally important. One needs and wants to be wanted, not to take part in some calculated expression of an extrinsic motive even if the motive is affection. When one partner participates, for the sake of the other's desire, in an nonpassionate although affectionate act of intercourse, the lack of mutual desire blights the unity of the couple. A monologue with a passive listener, even though a loving listener, poorly substitutes for an animated conversation. Nothing is more depressing than sacrificial accommodation. Thou shalt not be tepid is a basic marital commandment. In the realm of married sexuality, detachment represents a failure in charity. Rigid concepts of an ascetic spirituality based upon desirelessness has brought much corruption to Christian thinking on marriage. The negative way to God is not for the married.

So too, the old ideas in traditional morality about giving and demanding marriage rights are both ridiculous and offensive. If a marriage relationship has degenerated to the point of one person's demanding his sexual rights, then that marriage is so hopelessly awry that the merging bodies will effect little. As Paul Ricoeur has said of love in marriage, it cannot "be analyzed into a duty-debt. Its law . . . is the reciprocity of the gift."[5] Perhaps, at one point in the past, popular understandings of demanding marital rights, no refusal allowed, etc., helped justify sexuality to anxious couples. Basically, however, they also justified a serious deviation from the concept of marriage as incorporating mutual possession and mutual giving of rights. Since the one demanding was usually the husband and yet abstinence was the only way to avoid conception, there resulted much feminine suffering —and feminine masochism. Modern Christians, wrestling with subtle difficulties in obtaining unity of mood and a dynamic sexual harmony, can hardly imagine such a crude sexual universe so uncomfortably close to rape. But neither can they imagine themselves relishing a public hanging or auto-da-fé. The moral is obvious: sensitivities change from era to era.

Hopefully, as the reawakening of sexual sensitivity in our culture becomes more widespread, adolescent bravado and sexual overemphasis will also wither. The reaction to nineteenth-century puritanism can hardly last another decade. Marshall McLuhan predicts that as the hyper-male and hyper-female become less specialized, they will also become more human.[6] Life will become more erotic though less focused on genital sexuality; sex will merge with the rest of life as an integral activity. The only serious danger to our sexual renaissance comes from the culture's alienation of sex from love, emotion, and commitment. But the resiliency of man can overcome many destructive cultural forces. Along with eroticism, the ideals of commitment, love, even of chastity and romance, may stage a comeback. This time, however, the return would accompany a much more complex grasp of sexual reality. Tender concern could flourish; the playboy could become a man. Even in the present interim the potential for good marriages is greater than ever before. With taboos broken and women expected to develop as mature persons with mature human sexuality, married sexuality can be a greater bond and basis for unity. Despite the divorce rate (perhaps the price for a high ideal of marriage in a time of change), American marriages may be the most successful in history in combining love, sexual fulfillment, procreation, and companionship. People now expect to grow in marriage, not merely to endure.

The principle of sexual growth together should be as natural as that of intellectual growth and growth in parental responsibility and love. Because the sexual confrontation with one's self and another is so intimate, concrete, and encompassing, human sexuality can be dynamic, changing, and varied. As husband and wife grow and change in their married relationship, so will their expressive sexuality. But appropriating one's own body sexually while orienting it to another takes time. Each couple does this growing at their own pace and in their own way. Individual style varies with individuals; no ideal model exists. And sexual style may differ as much as Wagner differs from Mozart, as much as both differ from the blues. If the writers of sexual manuals tend to be Wagnerian, no matter; humankind adapts.

Those who too vigorously scorn marriage manuals, however, are not realistically assessing the culture. It may be an unaesthetic, cold, and repellent system to hand out books;

but then we do not perform sexual initiation rites at puberty, instructing the youngsters of the tribe, nor do we countenance initiation through affairs with older members of the group. Parental reserve balks at giving detailed instruction; church and school gradually and somewhat reluctantly assume responsibility. At the present time, therefore, technological, print-oriented man is appropriately supplied with instructions and information technically organized into print (T.V., or recordings for the children of the electronic age). The chaste, shy, and uninformed have no other morally acceptable access to correct information.

Romantics who rant against the desecration of technical instruction forget that they have been taught the biological facts somewhere and that their own passionate imaginations may carry them further than their duller brethren. Many of these protesters are extremely well educated and well read, and have already absorbed a broad knowledge of sexuality from literature. Those familiar with the Bible, Chaucer, or the modern novel should not begrudge the innocent their more direct, technical instruction. There are few who would not choose Boccaccio or Herrick over marriage experts such as Doctors Popenoe and Franzblau, but not everyone has this chance. The mechanization of manuals is a danger, especially in their quantifications; but ignorance and the rigidity of rumor damage human sexuality too. Man, whose sexual activity is rooted in his self-consciousness, needs cultural instruction. Spontaneous, noninstructed partners can suffer more traumatically than the mechanically misguided. More human Christian sexual instruction would fill a great need. In the midst of our current sexual revolution and/or renaissance, churches and schools must begin sex education well before marriage or even adolescence.

Christians, committed to doing everything for the glory of God, cannot omit erotic excellence from this "everything." A cultivated erotic sensibility may not always express a deep, passionate love; there are marriages in which the sexual relationship is excellent but in which other mutual relationships are terrible. But man is a body-mind unity, and a developed and enriched sexuality should help create enrichment in other areas of the relationship. Richness and variety at least sustain interest and forestall sexual boredom, one enemy of otherwise contented monogony. Our shriveled, stunted western sexuality may yet flower. Perhaps conditions of leisure and affluence can bring us to a culture where we work like American puritans and yet develop our erotic sensibilities. A couple should be capable of developing simultaneously the fulfillments of rationality and erotic sensibility. Sensuousness and intelligence can add dimensions to charity and create better marriages. As long as charity remains dominant, every sensible cultivation and development praises God. A welcome then to *Kama Sutra,* and may all the books locked away on all the special shelves be declassified.

This generation of Christians, with their newly awakened realization of the full dimensions of love and of Christian commitment to the world, may not have been able to avoid some creeping doubts about developing their married sexuality. After all, from St. Jerome to an erotic classic like *The Perfumed Garden* of Sheikh Nefzaoui is quite a trip to make in one generation. But human nature and love encourage generous passion and help to convince man that the good given to man by God includes sexuality. Not too much human reassurance is needed to deduce that God knows about sex and approves. Cultural shock and worry over perversion can fade away in "the liberty of the sons of God," just as worry over clean and unclean food withered in the early Church. The heterosexual-genital norm remains the goal, just as it does in physical and emotional maturity, but the freedom of play and joy embraces all the senses and sensations both for themselves and as an expression of affection. To delay and dally delights. Play refutes necessity and increases man's range and dimension. Pleasure, like the celebration of Sabbath rest, lifts man from the one-dimensional world of survival and necessity.

Trust in one's self and one's partner engenders an ardent sexual giving without hesitancy, a corollary to trust in God. The married can come to know God's joy in his creation as they learn to receive the blessing of marriage. Confidence overcomes embarrassment and reticence; one can learn to give extravagantly and receive overwhelming gifts. Married sexuality provides an expression in which physique, personality, and spirituality can become unified. While relationships still get "out of joint," the divisions and temptations do not by any means arise as desires over against rationality. Quite the contrary. To suppress sexual desire after a quarrel can be a moral failure—a cold, deliberate refusal to reconcile. The world can "end in ice, it will suffice," said Robert Frost. God has given man the fires of desire to warm the world; we flame in his honor as best we can.

The old religious objection that sexual passion interrupts inner mental devotion was built upon misunderstanding. The same mis-reasoning eventually brought intellectual work under reproach, too, for prayer and intense intellectual application are also incompatible. A serious under-evaluation of God's creation underlay the reproaches heaped upon worldly activity, which was seen as diverting man's attention away from God. Only when God was recognized as the author of intellect and creator of sexuality could these forms of self-giving and self-forgetfulness be seen as a human giving to God. Though dull, boring, repetitive work needs to be redeemed by constant meditation, the more free, creative, and joyous the activity, the more absorbing it is for its own sake. Good, absorbing activities become their own offering, punctuated only by short spontaneous prayers and sustained by margins of more formal meditation. Much prayer in the middle of study, during intense work or conversation, or in sexual intercourse would be like saying the rosary during Mass—a retreat or diversion from the immediate reality.

Several efforts at understanding married sexuality have elicited comparisons of sexual intercourse to the sacrament of the Eucharist. It is an illuminating analogy, although it does not satisfy completely. Both acts simultaneously create and show forth love, unity, and commitment; both also encompass the full range of psychophysical human reality. The biological reality of eating, digestion, and growth is necessary for survival and is accompanied by human emotions of trust, well-being, pleasure, and shared community. Incorporation on all semantic levels is a natural mode for growth and change, and the sacrament of the Eucharist works upon all human levels at once. But eating can also be perverted through unresolved basic aggressions and fears. Similarly, sexuality can be only exploitation of another. But, more often, the biological procreative process necessary for human survival achieves a fulfillment of instinctual desire while accompanying affection, love, self-giving, mutuality, joy. When conception occurs, a new community of three arises from the union of two.

In both Eucharist and sexual intercourse, primary, innate, human drive for survival and pleasure becomes as well a complex, involved, joyful celebration which actually creates new communal reality. Moreover, both Eucharist and intercourse, in expressing love, at the same time create and strengthen the communal bond. With subjective preparation and ardent assent, union is renewed with each coming-together. A Christian can live the Christian life without the Eucharist and the married man can live in abstinence, but both become a dry, deprived distortion of community. The recent Christian awakening to the importance of expressive love and community naturally reemphasizes communal Eucharistic participation *and* the importance of sexual expression in marriage.

As the monophysite, manichaean fog clears in the Church, the full humanity of Christ and of man gains importance. In the process much of the supernatural mystique about both the Eucharist and human sexuality fade. The small first communicant who is worried that Saint So-and-So died of ecstasy while receiving communion may also come to fear and overestimate sexual experience. Only the acceptance of total human life in its whole range of manifestations can obliterate mystiques of sacrament or sex.

It is, however, just in this matter of the range of human experience and emotions that the analogy of the Eucharist and married sexual intercourse breaks down and becomes unsatisfactory. In our distorted world, guilt and suffering impose a serious overtone on a communal meeting with God. Christians may celebrate the victory of the resurrection with pipe and cymbal, but the present exile and pilgrimage remain to be lived. The numbers and variety of people in the community of the Eucharist impose more concern and restraint. Some have sinned, some must suffer, all must die —the fulfillment of the kingdom has not yet come. The quality of play is strained, necessarily so. However, in the realm of married sexuality confined to an individual couple, the range and rhythm of expression may at times encompass all the joy, frivolity, and exuberance of the creation. There are limitations; there are times of sorrow, of mutual comforting. Yet pleasure in the sexual relationship does not have to carry each time the seriousness of all reality or always to bear the full weight of the communal situation of mankind. Eucharistic joy must confront and encompass thoughts of the cross, exile, poverty, the Dachaus of history, the Dauchau within. Intercourse, like the play of and with children, may often rest within the transitory moment of pure pleasure, "a green thought in a green shade." The long-term sexual community of the couple will involve enough seriousness and many moral confrontations; heavy burdens can better be taken up again after the re-creation of sexual pleasure.

An approach to the morality of married sexuality has been implicitly expressed in the above discussion of the lived marital reality. And, of course, all of the self-inhibitions of sexual behavior necessary for mature human growth as discussed in the previous chapter, also apply in marriage. Marital sexual expression must also be kept free from economic motives, from any aggression or use of force. Crude examples of these distortions of love and freedom rarely appear in marriage, but subtle misuse of power and pressure occur frequently. Men may pressure by threatening to stray elsewhere, women by bartering sexual favors for other desired ends. Both may allow immature self-centeredness, fantasies, or fears from the past to distort their growth in mutuality. There is no need to belabor the point that married sexuality which has the potential of heavenly fulfillment can also be a hell. When the other person becomes only a "function-bearer" for one's self without thought for his or her "alien dignity" as a person in his or her own right, grievous distortion enters married sexuality.[7] Mutuality requires two persons who are real to themselves and to each other.

Most questions of married sexual morality revolve around the attainment of loving mutuality and the continuities of the relationship through fidelity. Does the most mature, loving sexual community require absolute abstinence from all other sexual relationships? Previous Christian rationalizations for monogamous marriage seem to have operated under the principle that since sex with one was stain enough, more sex would simply increase the degree of corruption. The more abstinence either outside or within marriage, the more virtue. Even a modern religious author can naïvely say: "Undoubtedly virginity, implying perfect self-control, brings along with it all the other virtues."[8] The idea that sexual self-control solves all personality problems of love and virtue is ridiculous. Such a glorification of sexual control can be used to justify premarital and marital chastity only on the assumption of bitter suspicion and rejection of sexuality. Orthodox Christian doctrine following Christ's words does enjoin prohibition of genital sexuality for all but the married; but the justification for this standard is not inherently antisexual, as it may have seemed in historical apologetics.

The whole argument of this book has been that the ideal human fulfillment would be free sexual expression of all with all, but that sexual inhibition is a regrettable necessity of our limited human condition. The human limitations of existence in the space-time continuum, which is terminated by death and marred in this life by the inner divisions of sin, necessitates sexual self-limitation for the sake of development in time and living in community. Since humans have limited brains, limited nerve endings, limited muscles, limited emotional capacities, and a particular personal history in time and space, they cannot exert limitless energy in different directions simultaneously. Human survival, along with the wholeness, identity, and integrity of individual personalities, can only be achieved by alternating inhibition and release, alternating yes and no.

Erik Erikson's thesis that at each major developmental level the negative alternative must also be mastered is verified in the realities of life. Some mistrust[9] must be learned along with basic trust; and, more pertinently, the affirmations inherent in developing fidelity must accompany an ability to reject other alternatives. Surely this is part of the meaning of Christ's advocacy of the "narrow path" and "strait gate" leading to salvation. The man whose name is Legion, with his multiple desires leading him so many different ways, is very much in need of a cure. The very first glimmerings of self-consciousness in the child come from saying no and drawing a limit between what he is and does and everything else. Therefore, as discussed more fully in the previous chapter, sexual growth progresses by closing off alternative after alternative at different stages of development in order to channel attention and energy away from the family, the self, and one's own sex, toward the opposite sex, procreation, and humankind.

All in all, the main and most telling argument for monogamous marriage is not only that it is the best known system for procreating and rearing children (important as this is), but that monogamy fosters the development of wholeness and integrity and intensity of the individual human personality in a mutual relationship. The intensity of the sexual communication is provoked by the sexual exclusion of others. How could the Hindu ladies depicted on the temple friezes as engaging several lovers at once from all directions keep emotions and sensations focused with any intensity? Konrad Lorenz notes that close proximity of either man or animal results in hyper-aggression,[10] and human experience notes analagously that confined sexual expression results in concentrated and deepened love.

While the west may have succumbed to the romantic couple mystique, other cultures which countenance much promiscuity or even practice polygamy show a less developed sense of individualized personality with a less intense interaction in marital mutuality. Even when such cultures have subdued the sexually jealous Othello in every human, sexual indifference toward the individual is part of the price. After all, when one partner can repair at will to another wife or husband, there may be less conflict but there is also little incentive to master any mutual difficulties and progress to a new stage. Christian missionaries confronting a polygamous culture may make temporary concessions (remembering Abraham), but they should insist that a new generation work toward a higher personal idea of marriage.

The commitment to mutual personal fidelity enriches a

present sexual relationship by providing it with a unique private history and the promise of a unique future. The security and trust engendered by mutual fidelity frees the sexual expression of love. With a lifetime commitment, sexual love can be totally integrated, truly free, truly relaxed, and less troubled by temporary failures. None of these conditions are met outside of a permanent mutual commitment; there can be no premarital practicing before the complete commitment is made. If premarital affairs are sanctioned by society, they should not be called "trial marriages," for the distinctive characteristic of marriage in almost every human culture has been the hope and expectation of permanency. Only as a social structure crumbles does the commitment of marriage (along with all other human commitments) become trivial. Christians striving for the perfection of man and the human community must adhere to the importance of integrating word and deed, including sexual deed, with the uniquely human ability to promise and shape the future.

Fortunately, the highest human and religious cultural idea of monogamous sexual commitment finds some support in human nature. The paradoxical but interesting truth is that most men and women have a strong natural bent to monogamy, along with an equally natural promiscuous attraction to others. In nature some animals are monogamous, some promiscuous; adaptable man is both. The cultural and Christian commitment to the one-fleshness of man, a rational unity which transcends time and place, finds further support, however, in an innate shrinking from a division of sexual energies. Habit and the procreative drive, not to mention love and friendship, can easily keep the sexual drive focused on one person when the marriage is generally satisfactory. The primitive people of the world were apparently monogamous despite earlier theories of primitive group marriage. Practical considerations, along with slight forcing here and there, can keep the monogamous imagination intact. For many moderns, even in a divorce-torn land, the marital relationship may be having many ups-and-downs, even struggling through a dry period, but other sexual relationships are not completely compelling until all hope is lost.

Yes, despite his monogamous inclination, man does respond sexually to many others. Desire may spring spontaneously from the physical attractiveness of another, or it may follow admiration and friendship. Moralists and romanticists are horrified by these diverse inclinations; moralists deplore man's "perverse" promiscuous attractions, and romantics assert that since there is "one beloved" for each person, the one great love is betrayed by straying attractions. If, however, sexuality manifests a most intense self-consciousness and if the self is destined for communion with God and man (as posited in this synthesis), then attraction to others is natural. We are united through matter with all creation, and we are united as a species destined for an ultimate unity in one body in a new creation; these unities contribute to the natural drive of flesh to flesh, the attraction of persons for one another.

If we begin as "polymorphously perverse," delighting in

every human touch, and we end as members of one another in Christ, is it surprising that we hunger for one another on the way? The sudden desire or eruption of sexual longings which evade our usual inhibitions refers back to the biological mating drive and forward to all-embracing personal unity. Romantics are right to seee sexual attraction and romantic love as important and valuable forces in human development —if, that is, the romantic élan is not seen as confined to the couple. The couple should be seen, rather, as a stage in the ultimate unity of the body of mankind—just as love of self or of parents is a stage in the individual's ongoing genital development. Only in an earthly paradise, a paradise not found by our present human limitations, could we be continually "polymorphously perverse," generally genital, with all human longings satisfied without contradiction.

The doctrine of "complex marriage" propounded by John Humphrey Noyes and practiced by his utopian Oneida community was an instructive failure. All members shared property; all were married to one another. Since women had freedom to refuse, continuous courtship was necessary. Not only was sexual initiation practiced, but the man mastered *coitus reservatus*: prolonged intercourse without ejaculation but with satisfaction to both partners. Without the violent involuntary male climax, the community sexual life could be "a method of ordinary conversation and each married to all."[11] Such a cool view of community sex previews some aspects of the hippie movement, but both groups' rejection of the usual human necessities denies certain limits needed in human development.

The basic fallacy at Oneida, however, was in denying "the human condition," the reality of sin. Noyes pronounced himself eternally free from sin and so claimed the right to make eugenic decisions for his followers. Obviously, neither Noyes or his followers were perfect; they could not maintain a perfect love for all (just as the hippies cannot rid their love of elements of protest and aggression, as in "zap them with love"). Internal and external pressures destroyed the community, and private property and monogamy returned. Innate disharmony (call it "the human condition," "sin," or what you will), as well as the ordinary human time-space limitations, necessitates the limitations and inhibitions of monogamy. As a wise, married Anglican priest succinctly summed up our human sexual situation: "We will all most likely have a succession of Beatrices. That can be handled, and profitably. What is unmanageable is a succession of beds."[12]

Our Beatrices (of both sexes) bring richness to a number of our human relationships—a richness that all human relationships *should* possess. The so-called "overestimation of the sexual object" in so-called "infatuations" may be a norm of charity. However, to consummate each movement of love would mean a denial of the procreative community of marriage and a neglect of the promises of previous love. People do not fall in and out of love in a neat simultaneous rhythm. The human community, even a community with complete economic security, rests upon fidelity to promise despite emotional ups-and-downs. Desires which engender human communication and self-expression are natural and delightful;

but, this side of heaven, sublimation and self-inhibition are required for civilization and community. Sublimation by extension, rather than repression or indignant reaction, is the best method for overcoming temptations to exploit our own and/or others' sexuality. And such sublimation should be a calm and conscious process. It is helpful to imagine ourselves as the other with a past and future life or as (in the case of adultery) the other's spouse and children, and then to project our love and concern to the larger community of man. Healthy self-inhibition springs from a more inclusive affirmation, a strong concern for others.

The Christian attitude toward sexuality that insists on its relativity in creation as well as its importance in personal development and expression makes sublimation for the greater good an easier possibility. As already discussed in detail in an earlier chapter, Christian celibacy is one witness to the relativity of sexual expression; dedicated celibacy helps to develop an ideal of self-giving and sacrifice for the sake of others apart from sexual fulfillment. Another witness of the Christian attitude is the traditional acceptance of the fact that the marriage bond itself is broken by death. Widows in the community of the early Church have specific respected functions, and neither in those times nor our own are they expected to jump on their husband's funeral pyre. Christian marriage must manage the difficult stance of being a permanent commitment for life, yet relative in the eternal scheme of things. A person is not sexually faithful because of a mystique of sexual ownership or exclusiveness, but because sexual exclusiveness manifests a personal promise and integrated commitment pleasing to the God of Promise.

Those arguing for a relaxation of the Catholic prohibition of remarriage after divorce stress even greater emphasis on the relativity of marriage. They argue that just as physical death releases the marriage bond, there can be spiritual and psychological deaths that sever the marital relationship. The Church already recognizes that in many cases a marriage was never made, that a couple can be intrinsically incapable of joining themselves in marriage. So too, argue the proponents of this extended interpretation, cannot situations exist in which the death of the marital relationship is more final than the physical death of one or other of the partners? If the widowed can remarry, cannot the deserted? After all, the sexual relationship is not a "divine" activity, but a "human" expression.

Theologians must wrestle with this difficult moral problem in much anguish. Since man is a psychic-physical unity, it is dangerous to ignore or gloss over either aspect. Physical death is death, and there is no difficulty with its finality. But people can recover from the "death" of alcoholism or mental illness; they can come back from far countries and be reunited with family that waits for them. The very value of commitment and promise in human relationships resides in their qualities to maintain and sustain those relationships through difficult and hopeless situations. God, the Faithful One, carries the sinner through a thousand desertions. Should not man at least aspire to this perfection? Socially, thousands of marriages have pulled through crises and sickness because of the finality of the union. The impossibility of remarriage roots a couple in the concrete situation, focusing energy on working out their problems rather than moving on or retreating from difficulties. Charity hopes all things and sometimes accomplishes them.

Perhaps the Church could continue to insist on the imperatives of Christian commitment and fidelity while balancing them with some accommodation and mercy for the truly overburdened, for cases where no remarriage would seem to be destructive (as, perhaps, for a lone parent raising young children). If "invalid" lone second marriages were neither recognized as sacraments nor automatically labeled as adultery, a compromise between ideal and reality might be achieved. The partners in such a second marriage would then not be denied the sacraments, a decent social status, and general acceptance in the Christian community. Somehow, both Christ's call to perfection and his mercy for those stumbling over and under the difficulties of life must be embodied in Church discipline. Those who are involved in the most complicated and distressing marriage situations are surely among those who most need the strengthening and inspiration of the Eucharist. Christ ministered to sinners; he sought out the lost and straying sheep. Can his Church presume to make moral health a requirement for healing?

NOTES

[1] Cf. E. Schillebeeckx, O.P., *Marriage: Human Reality and Saving Mystery*, Sheed & Ward, New York, 1965.

[2] William F. Lynch, *Images of Hope*, Mentor-Omega, New York, 1966, p. 56.

[3] Cf. William H. Masters and Virginia E. Johnson, *Human Sexual Response*, Little, Brown, Boston, 1966, pp. 273-285.

[4] Mirra Komarovsky, *Blue-Collar Marriage*, Vintage Books, New York, 1967, p. 84.

[5] Paul Ricoeur, "Wonder, Eroticism, and Enigma," *Cross Currents*, Spring 1964, Vol. XIV, No. 2, p. 141.

[6] Marshall McLuhan and George Leonard, "The Future of Sex," *Look*, July 25, 1967.

[7] Cf. Helmut Thielicke, *The Ethics of Sex*, Harper, New York, 1964, p. 24.

[8] Cf. Lucien Legrand, *The Biblical Doctrine of Virginity*, Sheed & Ward, New York, 1963.

[9] Cf. Erik Erikson, *Childhood and Society*, 2nd ed., Norton, New York, 1963.

[10] Cf. Konrad Lorenz, *On Aggression*, Harcourt, New York, 1966.

[11] Peter Fryer, *The Birth Controllers*, Stein and Day, New York, 1966, p. 135.

[12] Robert F. Capon, *Bed and Board*, Simon and Schuster, New York, 1965, p. 82.

V

Procreation and Control

No SINGLE factor has been a greater stimulus in the Christian search for a new approach to human sexuality than the birth control crisis, which has introduced new areas of decision and responsibility to individuals and societies. The new freedom of man, manifested in the new attitudes toward Christian celibacy and Christian marriage, must also be explored in the realm of man's ability to control fertility. Should not the man who controls his own sexual expression now begin to control the results of human sexual activity? At this point in our discussion, many of the themes of the previous chapters crest, demanding practical and theoretical solutions. The argument of the first four chapters of this book has been directed toward a discriminating and enthusiastic Christian affirmation of the body-person, with a realistic appreciation of the irrational, as well as a recognition of the necessity for certain rational inhibitions, all for the sake of communal and individual development. With procreation, the communal involvement becomes paramount.

Conceiving, bearing, and rearing children is the ultimate communal action. The individual heritages of two people are joined in a unique new creation; all the physical, material, and psychic resources of both parents and of the larger community are needed. However, this communal social process of procreation and child-rearing has often been discussed in a misleading context. Labeling procreation as "rational," the "duty" of married people, is misleading both biologically and emotionally. Man's drive to reproduce himself may be less strong than the reproductive instinct in animals and less tied to mating, but it does exist. Distinctively human emotions reinforce the primitive drive for offspring. Sensual delight in the physical presence of one's own child fuses with awe and delight in seeing the child's evolving mind and personality. Respect for individuality and personhood, wonder at the potential and development of human growth—these human responses give depth to the joy of peopling a uniquely created world of family and home. Parents create a continuously growing community wherein reciprocal love can be given and taken. Procreation is an instinctive pleasure, a joy, a delight, and a privilege—rather than a rational duty.

With divided man, however, every good drive is open to perversion. The drive for children is no exception. Children have been desired for all the wrong reasons, from self-aggrandizement and pride to revenge, economic security, economic gain. Freud suggested that one major psychic route to the desire for children was the sublimation of the early incest wish to have children by the beloved parent. This may well be a factor in development, but what is the source of this infantile irrational drive to procreate with the beloved parent? Man's mature sexual drive not only turns to beloved persons but becomes directed through desire and love to create and build future community. The "generativity" of Erikson's mature person most naturally comes to fruition through producing and rearing children. Despite the possible perversions, procreation joyfully fulfills man's individual and communal potential.

The writer of Genesis recognized the importance of procreation to man. Man holds his mandate from God to "increase and multiply and subdue the earth"; Abraham is promised descendants "numerous as the stars" as his reward for fidelity. This mandate and promise are not repeated in the New Testament, but the privilege, joy, and responsibility of procreation seem assumed. Christ tenderly accepted children, strongly affirmed their rights, and used images of child, childbearing, and family love in his teaching. His reference to the laboring woman's joy that a man has come into the world reveals his accord with the Jewish tradition. Conception, procreation, offspring—these are a blessing and privilege. Christ proclaimed as a portent of the horrors of the last times that the barren would rejoice in their barrenness. And it is only

Christ's appreciation of family life that made him praise those who would leave all to follow him; only for the sake of the kingdom would family life be transcended. Even among the earliest Christians, who expected the kingdom to come so soon, childbearing and child-rearing are assumed to be the married's privileged service of God. Successful child-rearing allowed both women and men to qualify for leadership in the early Church.

Yet, as happened so often in the development of Christian thought, a priori assumption and joyful privilege became transformed into dutiful obligation when faced with challenge from heresy and an alien culture. Pagan license and manichaean hatred of the flesh both denied man's procreative mandate, although for very different reasons. Moreover, the prevalence of infanticide and abortion elicited a Christian defense of innocent and defenseless life by emphasizing the duty to procreate and educate children in marriage. Finally, a revulsion at pagan selfishness and the influence of the manichaeans coalesced and triumphed.

Suspicion of all sexuality grew to such proportions that eventually procreation became the only acceptable motivation for intercourse in marriage, or, worse still, child-rearing became "the price paid" for indulgence in the flesh. Yet, ironically, the suspicion of sexuality and the desire to defend celibacy and angelic marriages delayed any formal dogmatic statement of the couple's moral obligation to procreate. The primary purpose of marriage was defined as the procreation and education of children, and one could not frustrate conception; but until very recently the married could be praised for heroic sanctity if they lived in complete abstinence without producing children. However, such niceties of distinction, or so much abstinence, rarely prevailed at the popular level of Christian thought and practice.

Tainted married sexuality thus became totally bound and subordinate to procreation. The more children (and/or—however paradoxically—the more abstinence), the more holy the marriage. Applying all the celibate norms for an unmarried spirituality (negative norms at that) to the situation of the married resulted in much distortion. And the older forms of categorical thought and analysis misfired particularly in coping with the dynamic interwoven relationships of family life. Each act of intercourse was analyzed as a single isolated occurrence (as it would be for the nonmarried or in a static rational dissection), each conception and childbirth considered apart from the context of the existing family. An underground mystical stream of Christian tradition might include earthly love in a mystical affirmation of creation and God's dynamic love, but, generally, abstinence and rationality were the reigning ideals.

This inadequate Christian view of dutiful sexuality and procreation was encouraged by general conditions in the developing western culture. The necessity of marriage as a stable institution, combined with the fact of the low survival rate of both children and adults, placed all the emphasis on achieving fertility and building up the family. Gradually, however, with the growth of scientific knowledge and industrialization, the cultural situation changed and is changing still. No longer do most parents live in a society in which few survive childhood and where those who do prove to be an economic asset. Now, rather, it is anticipated that children will consume family resources instead of helping the family economy. There has been a revolution of child-rearing standards over the generations, with increased recognition of the requirements of time, attention, and education. The Christian west discovered childhood in the late fourteenth and fifteenth century as children emerged from "the anonymity in which their slender chance of survival had maintained them."[1] Through raised expectations and educational demands, the pressures of successfully rearing a child have increased a hundredfold. At the same time, affluence and technology have been accompanied by certain breakdowns in stable community life. The individual couple, therefore, must meet greater economic, educational, moral, and psychological responsibilities to their children with less help. Children may never have been so enjoyed, valued, and understood, but this appreciation and understanding means that their need for family nurturing is seen more clearly. Those parents who are not exceptionally energetic and/or wealthy can also foresee that having more children may very well mean slighting the children they already have.

The technological revolution which created these new cultural conditions also produced new biological knowledge and consequent controls of sexuality and conception which challenge the old assumptions and methods of thought. Focusing on each sexual act in itself was more logical when the male semen was thought to contain the complete embryo, needing the female only for womb and blood. Female ovulation itself has been known for no longer than the age-span of the oldest members of our society. This one biological discovery radically changes our view of the nature of human fertility and sterility, and the implied norm of female sterility has not yet been fully considered. The increased life-span of modern women insures that for two-thirds of her life she will be absolutely sterile (not counting the twenty-some sterile days each month during her childbearing years.) Biologically, female sterility is more normative than fertility within the present life-span. Philosophically, therefore, individual acts of coitus cannot be as surely linked to conception when it is biologically known that repeated and continuous coitus is necessary to achieve conception within the varied and continuous human cycle of fertility and sterility. Moreover, with the further development of new hormonal controls of ovulation, a new dimension was added to the question of control. With "the pill," the growing challenge that widespread mechanical contraception had been giving to traditional Christian ideas became even more insistent.

The first moral problem that arose was the basic question of whether or not man should control his fertility at all. Should parents attempt to limit the number of children they would have? Intellectually and theologically, this had never been much of a problem; because the traditional option of marital abstinence, which would in one aspect of the old view be an ideal marriage anyway, would inevitably limit children. In the first theological gropings with the problem of overfertility, complete abstinence was given as the only acceptable answer for a distressed couple. However, in popular devotion or "folk Catholicism" a view of providence prevailed which made even abstinence seem presumptuous. God sent children to the married and God would provide for them; to control conception was to distrust God's providence. The same nonreasoning superstition that tolerated the medieval ordeal operated here; surely an all-powerful God would not let the innocent drown or the guilty burn, or, in the modern case, the newborn starve. Secondary causes, rationality, and man's responsibility for the world were rejected as inconsistent with true faith.

The new knowledge of the woman's fertile time of the month was ignored, and the "rhythm method" was generally rejected as less than fully Christian. In response to a group of French bishops, Rome ruled favorably on a form of the rhythm method in the last century, but the inadequacy of the method's biological basis kept the reluctant approval from spreading popularly. In twentieth-century America a small group of deeply motivated married couples enthusiastically embraced a mystique of casting themselves upon providence in their family life. Heroic sanctity was sought in marriage through having as many children as God sent and living in the poverty and total generosity of the evangelical life. It is not surprising that this movement was often accompanied by a back-to-the-land agrarianism and a general rejection of technology. The rural monastery with its unworldly and liturgical piety became the ideal model for the home. The first generation of these married laymen seeking perfection in their marriages and family life were excessive in their zeal (as were the first desert hermits). And they were mistaken in taking the contemplative or mendicant celibate vocation as a model for marital sanctity. Casting one's self upon providence is a different matter when you will not bear the consequences alone. A child's welfare cannot be sacrificed to his parents' search for sanctity.

The tendency to disregard the world and secondary causes was gradually seen as a temptation to false supernaturalism. Christ did not succumb to the temptation to ignore the law of gravity and cast himself from the pinnacle of the temple to obtain supernatural intervention. Eventually, man's knowledge of the body and the possibility of fertility control were seen as giving moral responsibility to man. Man must choose once he knows, for to knowingly ignore choice is a choice in itself. A changing attitude toward the world encouraged new interpretations of Christian responsibility. The realization that God made the world and gave it to man to subdue modified the traditional tendency to passive otherworldliness, and it could be seen that subduing the world could include controlling the increase of human beings. Logically, fertility control is as valid as death control or pain control or any taming of natural forces that man has achieved for the betterment of existing human life. Man is distinctively human just because he acts on himself and his world rather than being submerged in nature. When Christianity can be understood as a working-out of communal salvation, then a passive acceptance of human fertility (or infertility, for that matter) is not an adequate response.

For too long the awesome fact that a new child and immortal person comes into existence with each conception blinded man to the sad fact that in a disordered world the existing human beings in a family or a nation could be harmed by this new creation. Somehow, the fall of man which brought disorder to the world was not thought to apply to conceptions. An interesting analysis of the Genesis account of the fall, however, sees the punishment of Eve as including not only pain in childbirth but uncontrolled fertility in the "multiplying of conceptions."[2] In point of fact, the disorder in our world reaches all the highest goods that man knows—life, marriage, work, procreation. Christians called to restore all things in Christ are called to correct disorder and to work toward harmony, the harmony of man with his body, his community, and his environment. Man can and should control procreation for a higher good.

This implication of the teaching of the Church became clear when the Second Vatican Council confirmed an idea of responsible parenthood.[3] The council statement marked an acceptance and grasp of new realities by Christian authority. First, the Council recognized that the physical processes of nature have been so disordered that new pregnancies can be a real physical threat to the mother's health and life. This is a threat which she has a right to avoid for the sake of self-preservation. Secondly, the statement recognized that many social and psychological disorders are also beyond the control of the individual family and can make additional children a threat to the family's social health. Thirdly, a new recognition of social reality is matched by a new understanding of personal psychological reality, i.e., the psychic dimension of sexuality which benefits the love and unity of married couples in themselves and in their child-raising. In the Church's newest formulation, responsible Christian parenthood includes a high evaluation of the sexual relationship of the parents. Fertility control, therefore, must not damage the sexual unity of the parents. But how? The means to fertility control becomes the crucial theological question once the right and responsibility of parents to control fertility is granted.

Simply to grant the right of man to act on himself and nature does not begin to solve the difficulties of control. When, for instance, does control of others become a violation of their right to life and dignity? History and the present condition of man prove decisively that individuals and groups can control life and events in a totally destructive way. The triumphs of education, technology, and medicine are marred by violation and suppression of potential, destruction of the environment, and base exploitation of others including even death and torture. The use of nuclear weapons at Hiroshima and of napalm in Vietnam casts dark shadows over humanity's advances in mastering and controlling the world. Birth control affects no given human life, but what of the power man has to affect the living and the power he almost surely soon will have to biologically control the future of evolution? A primary insight of the Judeo-Christian tradition has been that power over others must be severely limited: Thou shalt not kill. Love defines limits, and wisdom discerns which things should be done and which would be better left undone for human growth and community. As Erik Erikson states the problem: "In our era of limitless technological expansion, therefore, the question will be what man can afford and decide *not* to use, *not* to invent and *not* to exploit—and yet save his identity."[4] Everything is not permitted to man; humans must not arrogate total certainty in the shaping of life. The agony of our times is to decide how far and how total is man's responsibility for the universe and human life.

What is the Christian witness in man's confrontation with his own power? Perhaps the basic affirmation should be that the processes of life, nature, and creation are basically good —wounded yes, in "bondage to decay," with aberrations and mischances, but still inherently good, still "waiting with eager longing," still "groaning in travail" for redemption and perfection. The processes of our environment are neither evil, totally corrupt, nor even neutral; rather, they are predisposed to potential value. Man has the mission to correct evils, restore and create harmony (even through frustrations of nature), and to improve and develop. But man's mission does not include destroying or extinguishing processes which in themselves are meant to support human fulfillment. To subdue the earth is not to destroy and to obliterate. Man should explore and colonize the moon, but not blow it up experimentally; hunt and eat animals, but not extinguish them; use trees for lumber and plants for food, but refrain from defoliating the earth. The rivers, forests, animals, and air are not to be destroyed and polluted.

The new scientific study of environment and ecology support the old moral and aesthetic appreciation of man's reciprocal relationship to the world. Nature is neither sacred, evil, nor neutral, but a flawed good capable of becoming better through human development. The body is good and can become transfigured; the new creation and the new man grow from the good beginning of the earlier creation. All things strain toward perfection, and it is man's role to dress, develop, and perfect the garden of the universe, pruning but not uprooting at will. But man is not to so revere the past that he annihilates himself before processes of life and takes no action for human good (as has been the tendency in eastern cultural patterns). Man must take the responsibility of decision, but with trust in the goodness of the given processes of creation, with respect for the past and openness to the future. Man must revere himself and trust himself just this side of destructive pride and arrogance. He is son and heir, but he cannot pretend to be lord and master.

Man, truly son and heir, cannot actively control himself as though he were a fruit fly. Julian Huxley may speak of "higher animals such as the fly or man," but this perspective is dubious. Starving but devout Indians who will not kill the rats destroying their crops carry the reverence for life too far. At the moment of conception, biological human life takes on a decisively different potential for becoming a unique, never-to-be-repeated manifestation of the human species. If God truly became man and redeemed humanity for a special destiny, or even if all that one accepts is the assumption that the human species is responsible for itself as a community and responsible for the world, then the earliest beginning of human life carrying the specifically human genetic codes in its cells calls for respect of its rights. Every living human being, including ourselves, began here. Our genes may not be sacred, but neither are they indifferent matter. If specific flaws can be rectified to remove congenital defects, fine. But to completely change and in effect completely control the whole life-process for the future would be presumptuous and dangerous. Who, after all, has the wisdom to choose for all?

One eminent scientist discussing these questions has distinguished "negative eugenics" from "positive eugenics." In an article entitled *Science and the Sanctity of Life,* Medawar affirms that since "fitness" in its most general sense depends on a nicely balanced coordination and interaction of genetic factors, itself the product of laborious and long-drawn-out evolution, it is impossible for man to set up a "scheme of mating . . . regulating the number of children each couple should be allowed or encouraged to have" to improve his genetic lot. The most man can do is piecemeal genetic engineering to eliminate "defects such as mongolism, haemophilia, galactosaemic, phenylketonuria and a hundred other hereditary abnormalities."[5] Progress is made genetically through populations rather than through individuals and individual families, so that only by discouraging those carrying recessive genetic effects from marrying each other could a better population ensue. Morally, this intervention seems a proper function of man's dominion, with respect for free persons and community rather than complete destructive control.

As part of this respect for process and person, however, the specifically human method of mating should not be discarded. Ideally, conception in humans should be free, personal, committed, and loving, so that procreation takes place in the context of two parents uniting their lives and their physical potential in pleasurable joy. To grow human embryos in a laboratory without coitus, without parental unity, commitments, joy, or concern violates the dignity of man as a personally conscious, desiring species. If man values his own species no more than the rabbit and chicken embryos he uses in a laboratory, then he refuses his unique status above animal life. The Nazi experiments with human potentiality were also performed in the name of scientific advancement, but in developing the ability to treat people as guinea pigs, the experimenters themselves became inhuman. Man with all his power and extensive freedom has not been given complete power, and especially not over other individuals or another community. He cannot assume the right to experiment with nonconsenting human organism in the same way as he experiments with animals or other living cells. Proposals for banks stocked with the frozen sperm of eugenically outstanding males borders on the monstrously inhuman. It can only be an inhuman mechanization of man that proceeds in the name of reason by removing emotions, desires, and pleasures from human activity.

Technical proficiency in the service of promoting conception in a human context of desire, however, is quite different. The process of conception can be bettered and deficiencies of nature corrected, so that parents who were sterile but have longed for children can now succeed in having them. Happily, scientific knowledge can thus serve the human value of the mutual love and desire of the couple who desire to procreate. But such is not the case with artificial insemination or any method of conception in which an anonymous donor substitutes for the husband, for this destroys the mutuality of human procreation. The wife's desire for the biological fulfillment of pregnancy and her biological heredity in the new person is granted at the expense of the husband's biological exclusion. Worse still, the donor detaches himself completely from all personal responsibility for his biological potential; it is the doctor performing the insemination who must make the eugenic decision and who bears the initial responsibility for any future incestuous alliances, any future resentment on the part of the husband, and any legal tangles of legitimacy before the law. Procreation becomes a female and medical prerogative, excluding male responsibility (a serious cultural regression). Adoption, which might seem a parallel case, is actually a mutual act in which both parents participate, in which each gives up biological fulfillment for the personal acceptance of a homeless child. But mutual personal choice is as important in nonphysical parenthood as it is in physical conception. With the increased numbers of institutional children who are deprived of family life, Christian couples might well give more consideration and encouragement to adoption as a particularly apt form of love and commitment to the community.

The testimony of Christian celibacy to the possibility of full personhood and community without sexual fulfillment or progeny helped to modify the earlier pagan and Jewish horror of sterility. When charity and unity must extend beyond kinship or racial ties, then biologically producing family as family is not all-important; building up the community becomes primary. Physical nonparenthood implies no diminution of personhood. The single, the widowed, the old, the child, the celibate—all share in the kingdom according to their relationship to God. Women have not ended their useful life after childbearing becomes physically impossible; female animals may not live beyond their reproductive capacity, but people do. In humans sexual desire serves the love and unity of the couple who must continue growing in their love, as well perhaps as continue to raise their younger children, long after further reproduction is impossible. Sterility is a natural occurrence in the couple's life after the wife's menopause and even at times during the earlier years of their marriage, as when the wife is nursing a child. Only when kinship groups are more important than general humanity does sterility become a fearful fate.

Why, then, should artificial medical sterilization be considered a forbidden mutilation of the person? Why has voluntary sterilization been so unacceptable as a form of control of conception? Of course, to sterilize without consent is a horrible violation of the individual person's rights over his body and its potential. When authority condones sterilization as a legal punishment and accepts legal judgment as to who is fit or unfit to procreate, then that society and its laws regress one step toward Nazi Germany. In the same way, when (as happened in the 1960's) an Italian theologian talks of the legitimacy of sterilizing the criminally insane, the Church moves back toward the Inquisition and the rack. The body is "for the Lord"; what we do to another we do to Christ. Those who countenance involuntary sterilization (or capital punishment) might well be shocked at the similar justifications for torture in Vietnam or Algeria. Can any community claim this much enforced right over any of its members? Christians, despite past guilt in assuming rights over another's body, must protest all forms of creeping totalitarianism which assume such a right.

Voluntary sterilization, on the other hand, is another matter. Essentially, voluntary sterilization in a woman does nothing more than quicken a natural and inevitable process of nature. Sterility is natural to a woman during most of her youth, and it is absolutely sure after a certain age. To end fertility for the good of the community, the immediate family, or the mother's health seems a rational function in subduing nature. Modern Christian moralists have never scrupled to approve Caesarian childbirth or the hurrying of childbirth by artificial means to insure the good of mother and child. Why should moral approval of earlier sterilization be such a different case? The Christian censure of sterilization has never been as strong as that against mechanical contraception, perhaps because of lack of knowledge or perhaps because of past lapses when the cutting off of a hand or other bodily mutilations were approved as punishments.

It is instructive to remember that in the recent controversy over transplanting organs the first reaction was to consider such removal of a healthy organ a forbidden mutilation. Finally, however, there arose an understanding that the principle of totality and intentional charity made the former definition of mutilation inadequate. The body has dignity and possesses a right to integrity, but not at the expense of the total organism. Christ himself spoke of laying down one's life for a friend and of casting out an eye in order to enter the kingdom of heaven. Cannot the potentiality of fertility likewise be voluntarily sacrificed to serve the greater whole? And is it not primarily the taboos and mystique that have surrounded sexuality—and made it "more sacred" than other potentialities—that have prevented acceptance of voluntary sterilization as a means of fertility control. Then too, in the past, procreation was considered a rational duty rather than a privileged right of human instinct and pleasure, and voluntary sterilization would be seen as social irresponsibility to the community. Now, however, the human species is no longer in danger of dying out, but rather in danger from the physical and psychological effects of overcrowding. In a country like India, suffering so desperately from overpopulation problems where famine decisively ends so many lives, should not—and even must not—man decisively end his own procreative potential for the good of others?

The sacrifice and decisive step of permanent sterilization would be foolish before a certain age and before procreative privileges in marriage had been exercised. But after a certain number of children and after a certain age, two married people should be able to accelerate the infertility which time will inevitably bring. The possibility of accidental death of one of the spouses or of children does not really present an objection; no loved person is replaceable through procreation. Nor would such sterility limit love and service to the community; physical procreation is only one form of generosity. Naturally, voluntary permanent sterilization would never be be an ideal, for no one relishes any permanent diminution of the body from baldness to toothlessness. However, sacrificing one capacity may better the whole in many situations.

To move to another specific case, the temporary sterility now easily achieved through chemical means has the very important advantage of being immediately reversible. Medically, oral contraceptives may yet prove to present dangers. Morally, however, as long as no new life is attacked, the totality principle again applies. The totality of the organism and the well-being of the family and community justify regulating fertility by increasing the time-span of the naturally occurring cycles of sterility. But first prohibitions of the moralists concerning the "pill" were based on extensions of the traditional reasoning and old assumptions. Primary and secondary ends of marriage were still distinguishsed, a distinction rejected, or at least ignored, by the Second Vatican Council.

In the first reactions to chemical contraception, as had been the case regarding mechanical contraception, the old awed prejudice against sexuality was still reinforced by bad biological assumptions of the rigid inseparability of coitus and conception and the need to justify the pleasure of sexuality by procreation. The basic assumption in which the old argument goes astray was well stated in one of the current analyses of the problem: "All the traditional arguments against contraception imply this inviolable God-given direction to new life in the sexual act and the sexual function; the difficulty is that they have not proved this, their major premise."[6] Why inviolable, why absolute? In the gospel, sex is no more sacrosanct than other important faculties of man. Centuries of heresy and pagan influence, however, created the taboo and mystique. And present-day conservatives, yielding to a reversal of thought on the evil of sex, have ended up again with a view of sex as "too good and too sacred" to be controlled by man. Thus, those seeking a change in the Church's teaching on contraception have been accused of giving in to sexual license and/or desecrating the mystic I-thou sacredness of the sexual relationship.

Misunderstandings and delays in the development of a new morality result when new technology and knowledge have deprived the traditional natural law arguments of a putative, static, stable order of nature to use as a base. A recent elaborate philosophical reinterpretation of the natural law argument assuming that procreation for the married is a substantive good not to be actively opposed[7] founders on the primary assumption that procreation is still a substantive good in an overcrowded world. The previous testimony of rational men to verify this assumption means little, since all rational men at one time or another have been misled. The past is not the present, much less the future. Human nature does change, as radically as man's physique has changed over the centuries. Abstract philosophical arguments must be grounded in the present concrete human situation —and must realize, among other things, the limitations of human reason and the importance of human emotion.

Timing, context, and motivation give varied meanings to objective acts. A married couple fulfills their privilege and obligation in expanding their love and their community in a life together. Each act of intercourse need not be open to procreation—as, indeed, it could not be biologically. Only the misinformed understanding of the time sequence of conception can so identify coitus and conception that to intend one without the other is seen as irrational. Conception may even take place days after intercourse. Coitus also serves the unity of the couple, and often a couple will need to serve unity without at the same time expanding their community through procreation. Even if overcrowding and tension may eventually reduce human fertility naturally through evolution, those in need today cannot wait. In fact, the more expanded the couple's love and responsibility, the more the couple may need to be unified without having more children as the result.

All methods of birth control based upon extended abstinence err in a crucial and often cruel contradiction. Just when a couple's resources are overstrained so that having more children would be irresponsible, then the strengthening bond of sexual unity is also taken away by abstinence. Furthermore, those with emotional stability, economic resources, good health, and helpful friends and family will be able to cope with more children and so avoid prolonged abstinence. On the other hand, while those who are poor in emotional resources, material goods, or physical health are those who should limit procreation, abstinence for them may remove the one remaining sustaining bond and resource of their marriage. Only the rich and insensitive can speak of any positive values in stifling what may be the one creative emotional expression and pleasure of those deprived of all other communication and community.

Moreover, the supposed self-discipline of prolonged voluntary abstinence is usually not helpful to the personality growth of the married. Illness, pregnancy, work, fatigue, and consideration for one's mate impose much necessary abstinence in which sexual desire is already sublimated. This discipline is inherent, necessary, and appropriate to the couple's life together, and is rather easily mastered by most mature loving people. However, when even more abstinence become the only means to avoid pregnancy, then abstinence can endanger the couple's unity. Even St. Paul warned that marital abstinence should not last too long, for fear of temptations to evil. The less strong are tempted to infidelity, solitary sexual fulfillment, or regression to more infantile satisfaction. The strong and independent who have worked hard to develop a unity in their common emotional bond are tempted to separate emotions and will and to overemphasize their independence. A little abstinence may be as refreshing and stimulating as silence is to speech, but too much suppression kills the desire for unity as the personality turns away from the source of frustration.

Complete abstinence in marriage can be all too easy after a certain amount of frustration. It is unfortunately true that "given sufficient motivation, it is possible to reduce frustration by reducing erotic tension."[8] But affectionate, independent, "friends," who can live in the same house without "erotic tension," do not encourage deep unity. Nor do they provide the proper climate in which to raise children well. Passionate parental love gives children a comforting sense of being transcended and excluded. "They don't live together just for me, so I don't have to live for them; I can grow up and make my own life." A strong erotic and romantic attachment of the parents to each other also provides the healthy, necessary frustration of the various infantile attachments which the child must outgrow to achieve psychic maturity. Moreover, sensing that his parents accept and share sensual sexual love helps a child accept his own sexuality and prepares him for his own marriage.

Children flourish in an aura of physical joy, relaxation, and openness. An atmosphere of uninhibited tenderness and delight in the flesh creates blooming infants, whereas the contrary atmosphere of family strain, irritability, repressed coolness and/or cerebral detachment withers a child. Also, it is well-known that when children are not played with tenderly, physically, and with delight, they become psychologically maimed and stunted (or even die). It is important that parents be open to expressions of joy and physical play with their children. At the same time, however, husband and wife must be so absorbed in their own relationship that the child is not subconsciously made into a substitute gratification.

In theory, the "rhythm method" of periodic abstinence would not create the tensions of complete abstinence. Control is affected through knowledge of the body's processes; the fertile time is ascertained, and abstinence provides an allowance of time so that sperm and egg cannot meet. In this method there is no irreversible and drastic change in the body, no chemically induced hormonal change, no spatial barrier to the male penetration, no interruption of coitus. Aesthetically and medically, rhythm far surpasses other methods of fertility control. When there is no interference in any bodily process, there can be no unfortunate side effects or disruption of functioning. And there is the happy absence of intrusive mechanical appliances or worrisome routines to be remembered.

Barriers of time are different from spatial barriers, contrary to one argument for contraception. The couple mutually effects this barrier, while a spatial barrier must be placed in or on one or another separate body and can be done without the knowledge or consent of the other. Only mutual decision about timing can control conception in the rhythm method. Control of the body through knowledge and will preserves a continuity and interested unity of man's psychic and physical potential. Margaret Mead felt that Samoan girls did not become pregnant during their affairs because of their ability to know instinctively their fertile times (like the promiscuous, primitive daughter who watched the moon in *Tobacco Road*). In voicing the hope that all birth control could be based on such a recovery of knowledge of the body, Margaret Mead expressed a very human preference for effective preventive knowledge rather than effective mechanical techniques. Father de Lestapis makes this same distinction between external "exogenous" techniques and the "endogenous" mastery of physiological functions of the organism.[9] He also hopes much from future developments and research into the resources of the human body-mind synthesis.

However, it is just our present lack of sure knowledge of the physiological functioning of female ovulation that makes the rhythm method inadequate and often psychically destructive. The relatively short time of actual fertility cannot yet be predicted with certainty. Thus, an extended period of abstinence is now necessary to allow for uncertainty and/or variation in ovulation cycles. A short period of abstinence determined as biologically necessary for actual control of fertility could be easily integrated into a loving sexual relationship; minor obstacles increase desire and add piquancy. But an extended period of abstinence that requires serious repression with the necessary efforts of avoidance can engender all of the personal and family problems of permanent abstinence discussed above. Often, when cycles are short and/or irregular, and particularly when the need to control fertility is urgent, the periods of abstinence required will far exceed the supposed general norm.

But by far the worst burden of the whole method at this time is the anxiety caused by the lack of simple sure prediction. Even if all the efforts of calculation and constant preoccupation with physical measurements are viewed as a part of human responsibility and growth toward physical self-knowledge, the anxiety over calculation becomes destructive. Without the confirmation of medical or laboratory analysis, there can be little assurance that ovulation has occurred. While couples may try to duplicate a laboratory approach, they cannot live under sequestered laboratory conditions, especially when small children upset every routine. The emotional and physical vicissitudes of our hectic mobile lives often upset the woman's cycle. And the greater the strain on their emotional and physical resources, the less successful a couple may be at the rhythm method.

Worry over the correctness of calculation destroys the confidence and relaxation so necessary in sexual relationships. Conflict and tension often arise; for while each feels the imperative to show sexual love for the partner, yet each fears to impose the burden of another pregnancy on their marriage and family. The "double bind" of two opposing obligations can become torturous. As the reasons for spacing children or limiting children become more serious, then the psychic drawbacks of anxiety increase along with the periods of abstinence. Finally, when the conclusion is reached that no more chances can be taken with one's health and the good of the family, the only alternatives become complete abstinence or the use of an effective contraceptive. With all their aesthetic drawbacks, medical hazards, and canonical unacceptability, the effective contraceptives provide the best known control of fertility without sacrificing the normative sexual relationship of marriage. Values concerning persons far outweigh these difficulties; people come before things, the whole before the part. Those who claim that a woman employing a diaphragm shuts off her innermost self to her husband romantically overrate sexuality in life and ignore the total context of married sexuality.

Until the time when a technical breakthrough would make rhythm infallible without weeks of abstinence or anxious calculations of physical variables, many couples in good conscience will choose mechanical or chemical contraception. Chemical and mechanical contraceptives for the good of the marriage and family may be seen as a regrettable necessity in the same category as insulin injections for diabetics, hearing aids, false teeth, organ transplants, plastic surgery, blood transfusions, or any other intrusion or frustration of nature for the good of the total organism and community life. While sexuality is more intimate and important to the personality than some other functions of the person because of human subjectivity, the possible distortions, perversions, and personality failures present in sexual relations do not depend simply on reproductive "success." Can the defenders of the old tradition really maintain that the physical "mutilation" or "deformation" they attribute to the use of contraceptives (to use more pejorative words than "regulation" or "control") would be more immoral than the "shutting off," separation, and suppression involved in complete sexual abstinence? Is it not only the special fear-awe-sacred mystique surrounding sexuality that justifies sacrificing personal communication and pleasure to an abstract principle of a static natural law?

With the demythologization of sex, tolerance of the effective mechanical and chemical contraceptives (which, of course, do not attack new life) can be integrated in a new synthesis which incorporates the best of the old values with the best of new. Generosity, respect for creation and procreation, love for each other and for children need not be destroyed. Technology now provides an exogenous fertility control to families for whom no endogenous methods yet known can work. In the very near future new knowledge may make mechanical and/or chemical contraception as obsolete as a stagecoach compared to a jet plane, but looking to the future does not solve the present difficulties. Nor should worry over future depravities bar present concessions and change. Allowance of mechanical contraception and sterilization does not imply approval of perversion. The procreative mode of intercourse is still the sign of fulfillment of a couple's physical and psychic communion. The very psychic and social discoveries which first caused the reevaluation of sexuality and criticized the reigning rational biologism fully support heterosexual genitality as a necessary expression of maturity. Most psychologists might say something similar to Freud's comment on nongenital forms of intercourse; "they degrade the love-relationship of two human beings from being a serious matter to an otiose diversion, attended neither by risk nor by spiritual participation."[10] Added to this testimony is the philosophical affirmation that the genital male-female giving and receiving in coitus is necessary as an aesthetic symbolic reality for the most complete expression of human love, mutuality, and communion. The biological rationale of the primacy of procreation is not the only bulwark against floods of moral and social chaos.

Fortunately, most Roman Catholic theologians who have reinvestigated and reexamined the question of birth control have been able to break out of the confining asumptions and fears which forbade all control of fertility other than abstinence. They have, of course, had to work through the taboo-mystique syndrome in which sexuality is feared and oversanctified. A new generation of Christian thinkers has struggled to a balanced view of sexuality which recognizes the importance of the totality of the individual organism and family as well as its consequent relationship to the adaptability, survival, and betterment of the human race as a whole.[11] The new knowledge of the body and of evolutionary theory has been accepted, and more and more of the old biological misunderstandings are being exorcised. Psychic and social reality has been given its due, along with the importance of human cultures. As a result of these theological reappraisals, the expert advice and petition to Church authority has been to "change the law," while the veiled and increasingly not-so-veiled theological advice to the laity has been to follow their Christian conscience if it leads them to use methods of birth control other than rhythm. As the controversy has progressed, fewer of the theologians have been able to deny the incomplete understanding of the traditional teaching and fewer in authority feel free to bind others to suffer from a dubious interpretation.

Many of the laity have announced that their reason and conscience enable them to reject past tradition and teaching which has in their opinion been inadequate. There is a definite division within the Church. The polls reveal that many more of the silent laity have simply begun using contraceptives and continued faithful attendance at Mass. Others see continuing and widespread doubt, apprehension, and general confusion as Catholics stumble about in the ruins of the *Romanità* synthesis. The birth control controversy is a symptom of many more serious problems, and it inaugurates many difficult decisions over control of lives. Objectively, the birth control battle within the Church is an interesting socio-religious phenomenon to observe, if rather complicated. One liberal assumption that progress and lay initiative is always right breaks down when one remembers those historical situations when the Church began by giving way to lay, secular pressure and ended by violating Christianity. The Inquisition, for instance, conformed to lay wishes and current theories; the popes of the time gave way, though only gradually; history has recorded the result. On the other hand, the classic example of the Church's eventual repeal of its condemnation of usury comes immediately to mind. And no one can deny that in recent past centuries the Church has advocated Christian manifestations of social justice. But how often has this been only after gradually giving in and belatedly admitting the Christian basis of the reform? The Church, in these same recent past centuries, has failed slaves, women, democrats, workers, and Jews.

In the present birth control crisis, many members of the hierarchy seem well on the way to failing the married couple, the Christian family, and the underdeveloped countries with population problems. At the Second Vatican Council many bishops voiced dissatisfaction with the old tradition. It seems that no major theologians support the traditional view; and from the published reports, an overwhelming majority of the special commission advising the pope on contraception also recommend change. With such knowledge, educated Catholics can more easily follow their conscience and can speak with weary wit of the ambiguous teaching on birth control as "the pope's problem." But official governments, the poor, and those needing guidance cannot know or operate by inside information or subtle theological distinctions; they must depend upon the stated law and clear policy of the Church. For the benefit of those who, in the present situation of confusion and doubt, are not able to make a decision of conscience on the matter of contraception and who will never read or are unable to interpret the theologians, the hierarchy must change the traditional ban on mechanical and oral contraceptives.

In our age of speed and communication the Church cannot rely on the time-span of several hundred years that witnessed the tactful withering of past anathemas. Inadequate teaching cannot be quietly buried or imperceptibly developed when thousands have participated in the debates and more thousands face daily decisions involving the disputed doctrine. Maintaining the Church community in the present age involves an honesty and openness and speed not necessary in the past. Respect for authority and the worldwide desire for unity is dissipated by petty diplomatic hedging and the clothing of concessions with confusion. To "save face" is pagan; Christians admit failures humbly before God and man.

After all, authority exists both to conserve the best of the old and to initiate the new, not to cling blindly to the false security of tradition. The perfect model and precedent for a change in the teaching about contraception occurred at the Council of Jerusalem in 51 A. D. The problem concerned the gentile converts and observance of the law. Christian converts from among the pharisees were insisting that the full law be obeyed—dietary laws and physical circumcision. Peter, however, protested at making trial of God by imposing a "burden that neither we nor our ancestors were strong enough to support." After much debate, as recorded in the Acts of the Apostles, it was "decided by the Holy Spirit and by ourselves not to saddle you with any burden beyond [the] essentials."[12] A few of the symbolically meaningful dietary laws were retained, a few rules which could be easily understood even by those who did not know the full law. Purity and virtue were not left solely in the mind and spirit; they were to be manifested in actual behavior. But physical behavior in itself could not bestow virtue, nor should man be subject to the "too heavy" burden of laws based on an older idea of ritual purity. Peter and the leaders of the early Church finally understood that the new law transcended the old criteria of what was to be "clean" and "unclean." May the successor to Peter and the present-day assembly of the elders of the Church be as wise in the resolution of the birth control controversy. Let authority proclaim change; let the elders of today's Church charge today's eager and willing laity with a new liberty which, in its new extension of interior demands, will be more challenging and fruitful than the old external law.

From the discussion in this chapter on procreation and control, sexuality and contraception, we see the beginnings of many new challenges. In facing the problems presented in controlling fertility, Christians can prepare for even more complicated decisions as man's ability to control life and evolution increases. The need to demythologize while remaining human becomes urgent. Rational, active, technological man must also develop a sense of human limitation and an appreciation of the inalienable dignity of each individual and his human emotions.

As static world-views and perceptions of man give way to an ideal of development and growth, the ideal of humanity evolves toward a synthesis of human love and human reason, joy, pleasure, receptivity, and self-sacrifice for the good of others. In the realm of human sexuality, how can the great Christian reappraisal and restoration in Christ exclude the understanding and acceptance that technical means of fertility control can be a part of man's mandate to subdue the world? Sexuality is not a special sacrosanct function; but it is one of man's very important human attributes, and one of the important means of knowing and loving himself and others. The acceptance of birth control proves that, like the Sabbath, sex is made for man; man is more important than his own reproductive functions.

NOTES

[1] Philippe Ariès, *Centuries of Childhood*, Vintage Books, New York, 1965, p. 40.

[2] Jane Furlong Cahill, "Contraception and Eve," *New Blackfriars*, June 1966.

[3] Pastoral Constitution on the Church in the Modern World, Part II, Ch. I, No. 50.

[4] Erik Erikson, *Insight and Responsibility*, Norton, New York, 1964, p. 126.

[5] P. B. Medawar, "Science and the Sanctity of Life," *Encounter*, December 1966, pp. 99, 101.

[6] Denis O'Callaghan, "The Evolving Theology of Marriage," *Clergy Review*, November 1966, p. 842.

[7] Cf. Germain G. Grisez, *Contraception and the Natural Law*, Bruce, Milwaukee, 1964.

[8] Grisez, *op. cit.*, p. 153. Dr. Grisez' faith that "partial irrationality is a partial abandonment of freedom" leads him to talk of the dangers of "the appeasement of sensuality" (p. 102).

[9] Stanislaus de Lestapis, "Sexuality and the Modern World," *Cross Currents*, Spring 1964, Vol. XIV, No. 2, p. 238.

[10] Sigmund Freud, *Sexuality and the Psychology of Love*, Collier Books, New York, 1963, p. 37.

[11] *Contraception and Holiness*, ed. by T. D. Roberts, Herder & Herder, New York, 1964; *What Modern Catholics Think about Birth Control*, ed. by William Birmingham, Signet Books, New York, 1964; John T. Noonan, Jr., *Contraception*, Harvard University Press, Cambridge, Mass., 1966; Louis Dupré, *Contraception and Catholics: A New Appraisal*, Helicon, Baltimore, 1964.

[12] Acts 15:28.

VI

Family Planning, Childbirth, and Child-rearing

MAN'S WIDESPREAD freedom to control procreation and fertility is very recent. Not too much thought, at least on a basis relative to the history of the race, has been given to the exercise of man's capacity to control reproduction. Why should people plan families? How should they exercise their power over sexuality and procreation? The answers to these questions arise from and affect attitudes toward childbirth and child-rearing; individual and group attitudes toward sexuality and sexual functioning are complexly interrelated in any culture. Before control was possible, man's submergence in the processes of sexuality tended to divert these attitudes from his direct awareness and keen consciousness. The old submergence more often fostered muted awe at the uncontrollable, resentment at being subject to necessity, a feeling of being overwhelmed as a free person.

Men and women groaned or praised God when children were conceived, but their sense of helplessness kept the possibility of fertility control from being seen as a personal capacity and function. Now, at the opposite extreme in many highly civilized groups, over-control and technical mechanization threaten the human quality of sexuality. The laboratory atmosphere of the bedroom extends to decisions in family planning. The horrors of helpless apathy and indifference to family planning can be equalled by the chill of calculations and planning so exact that humanity becomes suffocated in superrationality. A modern proponent of social planning, Paul Goodman, gives a wise warning about planning in general: "To pre-plan too thoroughly is to kill life; and the more subtle the theory, the more dangerous the attack. . . Though we cannot draw the lines 'a priori,' in every case there is something to plan for and much to refrain from planning for."[1]

In considering the new concept of responsible parenthood, the emphasis must be on human flexibility and adaptability to other humans and to the environment. As Bernard Häring has written, "The very word responsibility—response-ability —indicates there can be no question of arbitrariness or human autocracy."[2] Unfortunately, however, Christians are quite familiar with one kind of arbitrariness. In an arbitrary emphasis on Old Testament valuations of fecundity, Christians of many generations exaggerated the merit of having great numbers of children. Complex procreative problems and decisions were made easy by retreating to evaluation by quantification.

Catholic writing on family obligations and spirituality almost invariably made the mistake of using large numbers of children as a criterion of success. The more popular the treatise, the more children the norm. While opinions in theological journals suggested that with four children a couple had done their duty to the race, a more popular article might well bear the title "Six Are Not Enough." A number of children ideally nearing the dozen mark testified to the couple's generosity to God. Admittedly, the modern desire for so many children was primarily an American, post-World War II, middle-class-educated ideal. The poor had children whether they wanted to or not; and studies show that the poor had children from ignorance rather than from desire.[3] One study analyzing preferred family size found that while all Catholics desired more children than Protestants, who wanted more than Jews, only girls in Catholic women's colleges regularly desired families well over the general American ideal of between two and four.[4] The same investigators found that, in contrast to other ethnic groups among Catholics, middle-class Irish Catholics educated in Catholic colleges desired the most children of all. There appeared few correlations between fertility and personality or socioeconomic factors, but religion and education did make a difference, along with family attitudes toward woman's equality in the family structure and her employment or career plans.

Why have devout Catholics educated in Catholic schools desired many children? The complex reasons include some that are praiseworthy, some that are merely unfortunate. One underestimated reason has been (especially for women) a real sense of generously serving God and man through a vocation of childbearing and family life. Education in the humanities, with stress on the supreme value of human life and development, stirs up procreative desire. In procreation man can imitate and understand God's love of his creation. A Catholic consciousness of God's concern with creation, comparable to the attitude of the East European ghetto Jew, emphasized the view of procreation as participation in the divine work. To bring a new person into the world followed the divine mandate to increase and multiply. Some motivation in increasing the chosen people in the American promised land may also have influenced the more entrenched Irish immigrants, a people who remembered well famine and decimation under English tyranny. In fact, a pro-natal "front mentality" in a community which feels itself disadvantaged may be a real factor in a divided pluralistic society.[5] The hostility to birth control shown by some American Negro adherents of black power would conform to a "front mentality" and the desire to "outbreed the enemy."

In the totality of Christian thought, however, procreation cannot be a means to power or simply a matter of fulfilling desires for the joy of having and raising children. Neither, of course, should procreation be a private method of sanctification, a guilt-driven payment for sexual pleasure, and/or a payment of debts to the race (some of the more unfortunate masochistic motivations of Catholics). Rather, procreation is a social expression of loving trust. A couple trust in each other and their own capacities as parents. They trust in God's welcoming love of man and his sustaining care of the creation. Finally, they trust in their own history and their present time and culture. Extremely alienated people often refuse to bring a child into this world. Voluntary procreation manifests primary acceptance of the goodness of man and the creation. And, in its more developed stage, it shows forth reverence for the uniqueness and individuality of each personality. Another child is not just another generalized child, but a special, unique, and wonderful individual.

Mature generosity implies openness to others and willingness to share and expand love. Sexual expression reaches the most complete fulfillment of its potentiality when mutual love, pleasure, and procreation are effected simultaneously. A couple who would close off the possibility of procreation without serious reason would be stunting the potential of their relationship, displaying a distrust of life and each other. Only grim necessity or a strongly idealistic goal (such as Peace Corps service, finishing education, etc.) can prevent the distortions inherent in selfishly refusing the possibility of parenthood. Human relationships flourish best in active process and pursuit of goals which transcend the immediate relationship. Too much self-conscious togetherness and self-centered concern for adjustment already afflict many American marriages. While marriages can be overwhelmed by too much irresponsible fertility, too much postponement and hesitation to create a family also bespeaks immaturity. Sexuality and love must be open, inclusive, and social as well as private and exclusive.

Even heavy burdens in the present, whether of a material or emotional nature, are not always sufficient reason to postpone procreation. Part of the couple's trust in the future is their reasonable confidence that they can grow together in their capacity to love and, normally, to extend their love to and provide for a family. Without hope for growth and concrete impetus, growth may not take place. A young childless couple may find it difficult to envision themselves as parents; they become mature enough for the role partly by taking on the responsibility. The relationship between expectation and performance is, paradoxically, as obvious as it is subtle. The enthusiastic acceptance of an ideal and faith in one's ability to achieve are necessary to produce results. When one reaches the new stage, when one becomes the parent of the new child, one grows to meet the new situation.

An example of this growth might well be the third child in the family. Parental acceptance of this child worries the demographer but delights the pediatrician. The early parental mistakes with the first children have been outgrown; later children generally benefit from the relaxed skill and wisdom of experienced parents. According to one tentative thesis, the later children are also less conservative of the status quo than the culture-bearing first child; they are more open

to innovation in society. In this view, smaller families producing more first children might add to the conservative
characteristic of a society or culture.

An individual family, however, can be guided only tenta-
tively by tentative theses of social consequences. The same
tentativeness affects theories of child-spacing; individual personalities change the supposed advantages and disadvantages
of the child's relationship to his siblings. At this point, a
couple can be responsible for only so much. The human condition being what it is, individual vocations, private circumstances, and one's particular community become primary.
The decision of a rich family on a huge ranch in Wyoming is
made in a far different context than that of a poor Indian
family in the midst of famine. Those who claim that all
large families are always and everywhere immoral in the
present world population crisis have not proved their point
convincingly. They do not make clear the relationship of
private families to population or the relationship of different
populations patterns in different countries. Social factors are
complex, and it must be shown how a denial of procreation
in an affluent community can help raise the standard of living
in an overcrowded, starving country. And how do the countries who need and plead for a higher birthrate for their
economy fit into the world picture?

The Marxist criticism also carries weight; our capitalist
"system of production tends to spread the view that existing
ills have a single cause—the population problem."[6] If a rich
country were willing to deny itself luxuries, if the millions

spent on cosmetics, liquor, entertainment (or arms) were channeled to the needy nations, then it might make more sense to discourage the rich from childbearing. But even in the present situation the capable, educated, and affluent might need to be encouraged to produce more people who could serve the world community. Sobering worry that the educated and culturally productive will not contribute their share of human potential and resources to the next generation is not a groundless fear. It is not too long ago that college women were faulted for their low rate of child production as compared with the rest of the population. As one scientist notes, thirty years ago our western society "heard tell of a 'Twilight of Parenthood'" and wondered rather fearfully where it all would end."[7] Now the falling birthrate in America is welcomed, and the decline of large families among educated women is thought a good sign for the society.

It is the very complexity, newness, and variability of the problem that bring difficulties in relating demography to personal moral decisions. The local balance of community resources and population seems a more sure consideration. Where the local government gives mother-heroine medals to encourage large families or where it pleads for family limitation, these are representative of the community ideal and should be given realistic consideration. Persuasion, of course, should never become totalitarian governmental coercion; as in all other things, individual conscience remains inviolable. In the particular situation of affluent America, where the birthrate is now falling and where so little of the wealth is allocated to the public sector and so much to private luxury, a prior community concern of the middle classes should not have to be self-limitation. When children are rejected primarily because they disturb leisure activities, a civilization is declining. The poor need to have birth control; the rich need more concern with social justice and redistribution of income. Alva Myrdal, a Swedish planning expert, pinpoints the problem when he states that it is "difficult for people to keep two ideas in their heads at the same time, namely, that parenthood can be made voluntary and that society can remodel its very basis so that more children can still be welcomed."[8]

At this point, at least in the affluent nations of the western world, the Christian responsibility for decision-making in family planning rests more on individual obligations to the children one has and will have and to one's own personal vocation and development. In any country the more unselfish action might well be to adopt children without parents or home, but in the rich sectors of the world with stable or falling birthrates the option to have children is an open and generous one. The generous affirmation of new life calls for limitation only when the good of others is most probably at stake. And, as in the case of the children already in the family, the definition of "good" must include more than material or physical needs. Again, however, each case must be argued in its individual context; arbitrary or alarming slogans based upon numerical faith that the fewer children the better are also misguided.

The modern context insures that the present-day mobility of persons in neighborhoods, classes, and occupations means that the parents become more important than ever in sustaining the child's emotional needs for love and security; and to do this, they need a margin of family resources. In a crowded family the exhausting effort to physically care for the younger children can detract from the very different parental care necessary to launch the older ones. However, with household help and extra efforts and energy on the part of the parents, difficulties can be overcome in particular situations. Some children in some large families obtain all of the advantages and none of the disadvantages of size. Since each family is unique in its different personalities, energy levels, expectations, and economic resources, no general rule will apply. The decisions remain subtle and difficult.

One important ideal and requirement, however, is that the decisions of the couple are mutual. Much of the birth control movement has been marred by a certain antagonism toward the male. The advent of birth control has often been portrayed as the ultimate weapon to free women from bondage to men. Margaret Sanger published *The Woman Rebel* with the slogan "No Gods, no masters," while Dr. Anne Biezanek, the English birth control evangelist, proclaimed the pill's discovery as Mary's gift from heaven to free degraded women. Dr. Biezanek opened her birth control clinic on Mary's feast day and joined the ranks of those who consider their apostolate as the rescue of wives from male brutality.[9] If there is more to irresponsible male depravity in marriage than the fantasy of masochistic imaginations, then all the more reason that emphasis be placed on the couple in campaigns for family planning. Simply conceding that contraception is a feminine responsibility (or a male responsibility) fails to meet the problem. Procreative decisions should be joint and mutual, with contraception a means to further marital unity rather than a male or female weapon to be used against one's married partner.

Another complicated area of joint decision-making is the limiting of children for the sake of professional activities. As the National Council of Churches' *Statement of Responsible Parenthood (1961)* phrased it: "Vocation, or the service of the couple in society, is another high purpose through which 'the two become one.'" The commitment to work is valid and important, and so is the commitment to children. Up to a recent point in western middle-class culture, the conflict had been partially solved by a radical division of labor: the husband was committed to work and the wife only to the bearing and caring of the children. But as women become more educated, their talents and capabilities impel them to reject this dichotomy and to prepare themselves for work and commitments in the larger community. Thus, many couples now face one more factor in their decision-making: development of the wife's potential for work, career, or some form of commitment in the larger community. Efforts to combine family and careers for women mean careful spacing of children in most cases, and early limitation of fertility in many cases (again, always dependent upon individual situations and resources).

Responsible family planning, then, attempts to control fertility in order to serve the good of the wider community

as a whole, the family as a whole, and individual members
of the family. Obviously, every decision sacrifices some alternative action and often some other good. The choices are
usually more difficult for those with many talents, much
energy, and greater economic strength. Once some limit of
physical health, psychic energy, or economic viability has
been reached, the process of choice is simplified. There is a
degree beyond which self-sacrifice becomes suicide. Recognizing the nearness of that point, the Christian parent can
clearly and surely see to make the responsible decision.
Sanctity involves curbing the impulse to heroic imprudence
as well as judging and acting against one's selfish sloth. Admittedly, however, there seems to be a narrow path in
family planning between selfishness or cowardly over-calculation of future difficulties and irresponsible lack of care
and foresight. Discernment, judgment, balanced detachment,
and mature love guide parents best, but all of these qualities
take time to develop.

Unfortunately, since contraception is a relatively new
technical power given to man, there are as yet many failures
of technique. Human error, unconscious resistance, submerged desire for children, and mechanical failure account
for many surprising "unwanted" pregnancies in present-
day society. In such situations Christians can witness to their
faith that each person is sacred and that uncontrolled reality
is not without meaning or hope. Hope stresses the value of a
new life despite envisioned difficulties and acknowledges the
openness of the future. The Christian parent can surely agree

with the wisdom of an Erik Erikson who says, "One may well want to reconsider the relationship between the will to master totally, in any form, and the will to destroy."[10] In all but desperate cases, acceptance can bring peace and sturdy effort rather than resentment and resignation. Many longed-for babies have not brought more love and joy than those who started out life despite their parents' efforts at contraception. Parental ambivalence toward a new conception is normal in any case. Nonperfect humanity often cannot help shrinking from the unselfish efforts entailed in great enterprises. Accepting a child is not totally an emotional feeling; will and conscious decision to open the heart and mind to love and growth play a part. Slogans proclaiming the necessity that "every child must be a wanted child" are too simplistic. Expectation, effort, and attitude can determine much in the future; seemingly predictable disasters and problems do not always materialize in family life.

Christian hope in the midst of difficulties does not deny present realities to exclusively concentrate on the future, nor does it deny foresight and preparation in the present. Rather, Christian hope concentrates on the present while leaving the future open. Hopelessness can so close the future that the oppressive anxiety over failure helps bring it about. Those who expect and/or are expected to fail—as is, unfortunately, all too often the case with reprobate adults and culturally deprived children—usually do fail. Expectation, or faith, or hope, or morale, or belief, whatever is common to them all, shapes and sometimes stretches the physical and social limits

of reality. Recent experiments indicate that even rats perform better if the human experimenters think their given
rats are superior. Although a couple cannot "play providence" counting on hope and work to overcome all things,
they should develop some ability to "let go," thus manifesting
their basic acceptance of life. This can be difficult at times, because any astute analysis of the reality of this world of ours
informs us that the good do not always "prosper"; they
sometimes suffer, go bankrupt, have breakdowns, starve, or
founder totally in their family life. Planning, foresight, and
prudence try to avoid difficulties, but do not always succeed.
There are forces which crush individuals and families despite all their best efforts. Sometimes, however, the lilies-of-
the-fields approach also works. The poet Robert Graves says
that "money is something that appears when you need it,"
and he echoes the testimony of many who ended up—most
unexpectedly—with all the things they needed for their
families.

Generally, however, parents, in planning their family and
exercising their responsibility over procreation, must balance
a basic trust in the past, the future, and themselves with care,
effort, and foresight. Since each family lives a different
reality, each family must make its own unique decisions.
Numbers, rules, and blueprints are impossible; even ideals
can be misleading. Christ proclaimed that to receive and
nurture the little ones of this world was imperative. Love
must serve, but the power to decide when our children shall
be born and how many of them there will be gives a new

dimension to service. Man's growth in knowledge must be used to further man's growth in wisdom in a very new appropriation of "the liberty of the sons of God."

Once we do conceive our children, we begin a whole new process. We begin to be intimately involved with bringing others to their own whole self-appropriation. Pregnancy and childbirth begin the individual's initiation into the culture. Obviously, the adult communal sexual world shapes the beginning of a new life, but the initial experiences in each life also shape the individual adult. To what extent is still a point of argument. Not many would subscribe to definitive Adlerian birth traumas, but almost all could agree with Margaret Mead that it makes a difference if one comes into the world with a thud onto cold muddy ground in the bush. Moreover, it is by now almost common sense to see that as a person grows so spectacularly fast in infancy, the emotions and patterns of interpersonal relationships learned in this critical period will affect the rest of his human development. Much is learned before speech, through the more immediate media of tone, touch, taste, smell, and emotional aura. Lasting attitudes toward the body and its functions are initiated by the earliest mothering attitudes. In a way, the society's reactions to pregnancy, childbirth, and infancy test the cultural acceptance of the body and sexuality. This acceptance or nonacceptance pervades the later education of the young and the general tone of the society, thus invading the sexual lives of the next generation. As A. S. Neill of *Summer-*

hill fame succinctly puts it: "If sex is a dirty word in the nursery, it cannot be very clean in the wedding bed."[11]

Perhaps because each infant begins life with a woman as its whole world, acceptance of women and acceptance of the flesh and the world have become intertwined. All of the great Christian heresies and past distortions in the realm of sexuality have been accompanied by a suspicion of women and efforts to segregate them from the world of men. Augustine, who felt that he had sinned at his mother's breast, logically extended his deductions to antifeminine, antisexual conclusions. As we in America emerge from the recent Victorian bout of antisexuality, we see that America, with all of its playboys and sexual flamboyance, has not completely accepted the human body.

For a barometer reading of gnosticism, we can measure the amount of unease with which pregnant women are met, the emotional revulsion at the messiness and gore of childbirth, the embarrassment and discomfort at the sight of a nursing mother. These extremely sexual functions of women remind adults that sexual intercourse does take place and does produce children. Every man and woman alive was conceived, born, and in helpless need of his or her mother's physical care as well as her love, of her breast, of her cleansing and diapering. Such facts disturb the approved conventional role-playing of our American society in which all appear fully dressed, self-controlled, and self-sufficient. To a cool contained culture, the physical facts and intimacy of the processes of pregnancy, childbirth, and infancy are distasteful and best forgotten or ignored. Americans get nervous if another touches them or invades their three-foot-safe-distance perimeter; babies within the womb, at birth, or suckling at the breast simply get too close for comfort.

Is there not, however, a cultural correlation between changing attitudes toward sexuality and emotion in general and childbirth in particular. The proper lady who a generation or two ago only mentioned "limbs" and dared not hold a man's hand in public also retired from society during pregnancy. If she did go out, she wore dark-colored dresses five sizes too big, and surreptitiously went her embarrassed way. Today, with far less taboo in speech, dress, and behavior, women wear fashionable rainbow-colored, miniskirted maternity clothes that hide neither their knees nor the fact of their pregnancy. A society in which pregnancy does not arouse embarrassed joking or shame and in which pregnant women can remain attractive and physically evident progresses toward mature sexuality. The fear-reverence-shame reactions give way to a human acceptance of sexuality that also recognizes the primacy of personal identity in the woman. Gradually, the customs and laws governing the education, employment, and social life of pregnant women have become rational rather than emotional. Female pregnancy does not need to corrupt or disrupt campus, office, or beach. Ski slopes are usually forbidden, but the criterion is the well-being of the baby, not the delicate sensibilities of fellow skiers.

Developments in the managing of childbirth display the

same interesting correlation with attitudes toward women and sexuality. In the depths of the nineteenth century and its aftermath, nice women were supposed to abhor the violation and crudity of sexual intercourse. Ladies were not to "participate" but to "submit to the male," as befit their general cultural role. Without equality and mutuality, little pleasure and loving integration of sexuality within the personality was possible. Many women did become only submissive, and looked upon any participation in sexuality only as a dutiful sacrifice of themselves. Women's subjection and lack of freedom was accepted as part of the divinely appointed structure of the universe, Eve's punishment from God.

As a natural extension of this thinking, childbirth, with all the emphasis on its pain, agony, and danger, was seen as the culmination of the punishment of Eve. Even anesthesia was thought impermissible, since it would lessen the pain and the divinely sanctioned punishment of women and the race. Woman's true role was to submit to her fate; it was her duty to suffer. Naturally, too, she was also to submit to her doctor, whose ministrations in those days before the development of modern hygienic and medical knowledge were often faulty and even fatal. Then too, women weakened by physical and psychic undermining of their sexual life, by fear, and by inadequate care not surprisingly often proved unable to nurse their babies. It was not uncommon, therefore, to have recourse to the "wet nurse," who was often of hardy peasant stock, lower in the social scale, and so thought more capable of animal-like functions than the delicate middle-class lady. A dualism of the functioning sexual woman and the ideal nonsexual lady could be imbibed with one's non-mother's milk.

In America the next phase of development in attitudes toward childbirth (along with new attitudes toward sexuality) brought a high level of technical excellence in medical care and hygiene. Only in unusual cases did women or their babies die, nor were mother or child weakened from improper medical care. However, the price for this efficiency was a prevailing attitude that pregnancy was a disease which the doctor would cure with hygienic medical and surgical procedures, complete with drugs, instruments, and the complete passivity of his patient. Whereas women had once delivered their babies, now doctors delivered babies from unconscious female bodies. The preparation for this operation was paternal reassurance, a few instructions to be followed, and minimal attention to the patient's understanding or personal participation. Pregnancy and childbirth were to be painless nonexperiences managed by the doctor and the hospital staff. Mothers-to-be, even in normal noncomplicated cases, were treated as helpless patients who, after all of their clothes, jewelry (including their wedding rings), and all possessions were removed, were drugged and fittingly enough put in cribs. While the woman was conscious of nothing, remembered nothing, the doctor delivered the baby, who was whisked away to a nursery unseen, unrecognized, and untouched by his mother or father. Needless to say, the unconscious and inert mother was not to be seen by the banished father. Such a rigid system of technique, organization, efficiency, and hygiene could not help but erode human relationships, human meanings, marital mutuality, and woman's initiative; and who-knows-what with the baby? Of course, motivation is all, and the inhumanity of much of the vaunted technical progress in maternal care was directed toward the good of the mother and child understood in a detached, one-sided way. The technical ideal of the machine age is, after all, an efficient standardized assembly line of production; standardized maternal deliveries could not be so easily produced with personalities and personal relationships spoiling the precision.

In this whole technological approach, the natural function of breast-feeding was almost totally abandoned. Nursing a child is a unique mutual relationship which is very dependent upon the inter-personal responses involved. Maternal diet, rest, illness, immunities, and, above all, emotions, directly affect the baby. When the baby instinctively manifests its need, the mother's milk begins to flow; not to nurse can be painful. But this intimate physical interdependence seemed primitive to the first prophets of technique and efficiency, so the precision-made formula arrived. Anyone with the proper mechanical equipment and formula could take care of the baby. Women were told that they should not nurse, could not nurse, and in some cases were automatically given pills to dry up their milk without any prior consultation. The doctors (almost exclusively male, of course) who proclaimed that American women could not nurse their babies knew best. Any normal difficulties in the initial adjustments to nursing were often used to pressure women to give it up. And the fact that nursing gives mild sexual pleasure increased the anxiety of women who had been taught to reject their body and their sexuality.

However, with the sexual revolution, a new generation of sexually emancipated women has grown up who have demanded more participation in childbirth and returned to nursing their children. Once active sexual functioning becomes accepted in a woman's self-image, pleasure and desire accompany all aspects of voluntary procreation. Women who have achieved this self-image wish to consciously bear their own babies, to have the support and company of their husbands at this time, and to nurse their children. Since these women are usually educated, independent, and freely affirming their feminine functions, they do not relish an assembly-line approach based upon unquestioning submission to authority, conformity, and routine. Why should normal childbearing become separated from personal identity and the marriage relationship? Male medical authority can no longer count on its mystique to impose compliance. A new generation of doctors (female as well as male) have begun to educate mothers, to see them as co-workers in bringing forth a healthy baby. Ironically, drugs which began as a help to women (and still can be) have also become an aggressive weapon of medical control when used without the mother's consent. Rarely do emergency situations create the need for an active dominant battle for life in childbirth, yet many a medical professional cannot give up this active model to act in ordinary cases as a supporting co-worker with the mother. Like feminine orgasm, suffrage, and education, feminine participation and assertion of personhood in childbirth upsets the old order of masculine dominance and control.

Conditioning women's brains and muscles so that a normal birth can be consciously experienced, with little pain or only mild discomfort, does mean, of course, spending time and effort in instructing and training women. Through trained mental conditioning and breath and muscle control, women can also control the interpretation of the sense data in the brain. With conditioning and detailed knowledge of the process of childbirth, women can work with their body's automatic process to facilitate labor and delivery. Sensations which in an anxious, disorganized physical and psychic state are felt as excruciatingly painful are felt only as violent physical effort to the conditioned woman who remains a person in active control. She labors hard, but not in a passive anguish of pain and anxiety. The resulting sense of achievement when her child is born can produce a natural ecstasy and euphoria remembered for a lifetime. Those who compare such a childbirth to orgasm are not far wrong, and perhaps new mothers who are frustrated in missing this experience do suffer depression from their lack of fulfillment.[12] With alert conscious birth, the baby can be touched and held and given human caresses immediately, before being "cleaned up" and made presentable. Recognition and mutual sensation can give a good beginning to the mother-child relationship, and it is even more desirable if the father can also see and hold the child.

How odd it seems, in a detached view, that our recent cultural patterns have so deprived mothers and fathers in greeting their own child. A whole process of disassociating sexuality from life and human emotions was thus encouraged at birth. No wonder adults in our culture find it difficult to appropriate their own bodies and integrate sexuality into their personality. Now, however, new approaches and attitudes indicate an enlightened change. As Erikson says, American puritanism "spreading its frigidity over the tasks of pregnancy, childbirth, nursing, and training . . . compromising all sensuality," can begin to be reversed in a new era with methods such as "natural" childbirth; trained, prepared childbirth's "reintroduction represents a judicious mixture of eternally natural and progressively technical methods" in the service of human life.[13] Efforts to humanize birth and infant care are a beginning step in the acceptance and personalization of pleasureable sexuality. A culture's sexual renaissance begins in infancy.

The fact that every human life begins in conception, pregnancy, and childbirth presents a unique challenge in the human condition. Due to the inner division of man, an inherent inertia gives a residual *non serviam* which can take the form of resistance to passion or even to a strongly desired pregnancy. A woman can go through sexual intercourse or an entire pregnancy separated from the process and/or

fighting it. Usually, however, women, along with Margaret
Fuller, "accept the universe." Many come to accept and
affirm; and the modern woman is coming, not only to accept
and affirm, but to "make love" and procreate with active
intensity and pleasure. Pregnancy and childbirth present a
rare opportunity to integrate human consciousness, will, and
love with biological processes. Theologians tell us death is
also such a rendering choice before biological processes, and
it may well be. Certainly, however, women in pregnancy and
childbirth can confront much experience in a compressed
time-span. They get a remembrance of growing up and at
least a preview of aging, for they know their body to change
before their eyes whether they would or no. This fact is well
noted in Pasternak's modern classic *Doctor Zhivago,* wherein
the hero discerns the pregnancy of his Lara because he feels
that, like all women first pregnant, her face has a disoriented
blurred look. As in adolescence, the unknown biological potential and speed of change can be overwhelming. With
affirmation and direction toward the future comes the blooming look in a healthy pregnant woman, the euphoria of the
self-knowledge that identity will be enhanced by this gift
of self to a new life.

Simone de Beauvoir, in calling the child within "a para-
site," rejects the central reality of a love which grows
through giving and receiving. Her talk of women enslaved
to the species misses the central fact that "the species" is in
every case an abstract word standing for living fellow human
beings and, in the case of pregnancy, for one unique human

incarnation within. A human freedom which would be as the gods and never give through the flesh, never accept community and continuity into the future beyond the present —this human freedom excludes love. If the claim is correct that many women come to greater wisdom and learn to love better earlier in life than men do, at least a partial basis for this claim may be attributed to the opportunity given to many women to reflect and grow through their experience in childbearing. It is less usual for men to experience in early life a comparable opportunity for growth in self-giving through reflection. There are notable exceptions, of course, as witnessed in the self-growth of great men through periods of illness or imprisonment. Unfortunately, however, the more usual youthful challenge for males has been war, an effort and self-giving that presupposes violent destruction of fellow human beings. How much better if mankind as a whole could take the procreative childbearing model of self-giving and labor to transform necessity in the cause of life, love, and growth.

Western Christianity can remember with hope and thankfulness that it has always used procreative images to describe its communal life. The Church is seen as a woman with child, and Christ specifically compared the coming of the kingdom to the labor and joy of childbirth. Paul also uses this image, picturing himself in travail to bring forth his church community who then must be nourished with the milk of doctrine. Human birth and growth are like the other hidden processes in which seeds "die to grow"—mustard seeds become trees; leaven leavens. These images of birth and gradual development assume that each human birth begins a unique concrete history in a future-directed flow of time. The Christian birth of the new man through baptism becomes a part of collective salvation history only because concrete individuals are born and interact with one another. Christian redemption must affect this concrete world, these specific births and life-cycles, these known relationships and realities.

The fall of man and man's consequent radical problems with living are also far from the abstractions of theology. As Genesis so aptly summed them up, man's work for survival is hard; men and women's relationships are distorted; women have troubles with conception and travail in childbirth; and every human being faces the inevitability of death. The beginning of life, the end of life, and the in-between are beset with difficulties. But the Good News of the gospel, of Christian rebirth, confronts the pain and struggle of life; and all progress in alleviating the effects of the fall upon the world God so loved are worthy of Christian effort. The whole concern of this book has been to affirm the growth of man's participation in redemption, specifically in the justification and desirability of man's overcoming the sexual distortion in the Genesis story. Theologians can now realize that after the redemption the subordination of women and their pain in childbirth (which have so distorted all of human sexuality) are not immutable conditions of life. Pope Pius

XII spoke of Genesis' curse of pain in childbirth as a descriptive analysis of the human condition, not as God's mandate for passive suffering. Methods of instructing and conditioning women for childbirth which could help to eliminate pain were evaluated by Pius as Christian and humanizing efforts to subdue the world. Moreover, truth being truth, the fact that these methods evolved from the Russian scientist Pavlov's research and were developed in communist countries does not discredit them. Marxist materialists, taking matter seriously (for once) and committed to the dignity of labor, have pioneered in humanizing birth in a way which may lead to other restorations of sexuality.

Why have not "Christian materialists" emerged? Why have modern Christians not developed more humane concerns while supposedly affirming the creation, incarnation, and resurrection? The misuse and misinterpretation of the events of Christ's birth and resurrection have played their part. In the gospel accounts of Christ's infancy, the emphasis was put on Mary's virginal conception rather than God-be-come-embryo. What could have been an overwhelming affirmation of matter, process, and biological reality was instead interpreted as a denial of sexuality and the body. A real woman great with a real child receded behind the awe of miraculous nonsexual conception. And any future nonmiraculous pregnancies of Mary were denied on the sole basis of introducing desecration to her dignity. Now that man can induce parthenogenesis in rabbits and frogs, our interest in the miraculous element of the virgin birth has waned. Our awe and attention now concentrate on the implications of God entering his creation in human history as a human person no matter how.

Yet, if a new creation has begun with Christ's incarnation, the biological laws of the old ways of life and death are intrinsically affected. If a new heaven, a new earth, a new life, and the resurrection of the body are results of the redemption, then the radical newness infused in the primary life-process of a virgin birth is an apt beginning for a new and different bodily existence. Even as a miracle, the virgin birth is perfectly balanced with immanence and transcendence: the evolution of the human species is irrevocably and irreversibly combined with a totally new power and potential through the primary and basic human developmental process in the womb. And, whether emphasizing or minimizing the miraculous, angels, shepherds, star, and wise men cannot alter the basic acceptance of the hidden irrational world of womb, breast, and infancy that precedes every adulthood. The infancy gospels and the basic Marian doctrines affirm that creation and human nature have been included in redemption.

Anyone who has read psychoanalytical works treating the mother's effect on her infant child can accept the need for a special mother to produce a special son; the concept of the holy family with a new and different mother-child, father-son, husband-wife relationship is not irrelevant to the modern mind. Unfortunately, however, the infancy gospels and a rigid ideal of "the holy family" were used and elaborated on all too extensively in past centuries to deny the body, sexuality, and creation. Late legends of a supermiraculous birth furthered denials of the body in general and of women's sexual functioning in particular. Stories which had the infant Jesus suddenly materialize in Mary's arms or pass through closed flesh resulted from the attitudes of those who felt the feminine processes of birth to be unclean and incompatible with personal integrity. According to Karl Rahner, a few early theologians, "in express terms, reject an afterbirth as unfitting."[14] The cultural correlation of attitudes toward sex and childbirth again apply; when sexual openness to another was denied as an expression of love, when women were held in contempt, then Mary's participation in the normal processes of a real childbirth was also denied.

This tradition might have been interpreted in a completely different vein. Mary's painless birthing of Christ could serve as the redemptive affirmation of women, their sexuality, and their procreative role. Through Mary's active childbirth of joy, one of the effects of the fall of man could be seen as removed. The ideal of the virgin who painlessly gave birth—"As if she were a man, Of her own will," as expressed in one second-century ode[15]—could be a sign of the full restoration of the dignity of women. In the new creation women were not to be subject to the dominion of men or to suffer pain in the procreative function. With Christ's advent, the inequality and division of the sexes would be overcome. Women's childbearing could be transformed through active free consent, restoring her physical integrity and banishing pain if not effort. Mary's totally free, knowing consent to pregnancy was perhaps the first such consent in the human species; if so, this special wholeness was a fitting prelude to the restoration of freedom for humankind.

Just as the infant Jesus was to initiate the discovery of childhood in the Christian west,[16] so Mary's free consent and active birthing initiate free parenthood and the unity of mind and body processes. Such an integrity and unity of conscious and unconscious human processes can be coveted, not only by every believer's "fiat," but also by those now procreating new life. Inspired by the way God has dealt with us, we try as a group and as individual parents to call forth wholeness in our children. Beginning with a birth that is as fully human and personal as we can make it, we continue the effort to bring up integrated human beings while changing the culture we and they will live in.

It must be noted, however, that one cannot hope to produce loving, adequate, sexually integrated persons in an environment that denies the social conditions required to produce and sustain loving, adequate people. Without peace, economic security, health care, housing, intellectual stimulation, and moral concern, sexual life will be distorted along with the rest of human potential. Society and the communities within it must change before the individual members can develop fully. Social revolutionaries make a good case against sexual reformers who ignore the social and economic facts of life. Jobs, money, housing, education, and peace are basic.

Yet it remains true that man does not live by bread alone; emotional growth and abilities to sustain human relationships are also necessary for social reform. Stunted personalities do not make revolutionaries, nor do grasping elites reform.

Cultural patterns of giving and getting, self-images and structures of response—all are influenced by sexual development, beginning with the earliest preverbal learning through the body and the emotions. Negative proof of the effects of early interpersonal influences abound in our world today, from the experience of wartime abandonment of children to the absence of fathers in deprived ghettos. Preverbal class distinction destines many children to a limited life. Progress in society and communities can come only gradually through the changes in each new generation. Total revolution seems unlikely in our western world, and the cataclysm of nuclear war would leave only a few alive. Our reforms and social changes will come about with changes in opinion, education, and behavior. Our present so-called sexual revolution began with a new openness in attitudes in the 1920's, new marriage patterns, and new theories of child-rearing. Permissive positive approaches to human nature did not just descend from the mushroom cloud or sprout with the Sputnik's. Cultural historians delight in digging out the genealogies of "new" ideas; but it is safe to say that our own modifications will be affecting our grandchildren as well as our children. Therefore, we try and try again for wholeness in each stage of the child's development.

The acceptance of the human body implicit in an affirmation of childbirth and nursing must become explicit to the infant child. Communication through touch, tone, food, warmth, smell, and emotional auras can convey to him a sense of euphoria; he is pleasing and highly valued. The baby smiles and elicits smiles; to give and receive pleasure sustains life, just as to learn and affect the environment does. Play, pleasure-filled and loving care, give babies the early self-acceptance needed for sexual integrity. Acceptance and stimulation by the human family make human beings human. Regretably, however, the introduction to the human community also requires inhibition; humans inhibiting other humans usually impress some degree of anxiety and shame. The vulnerable child is dependent on the accepting emotions of others, and he can learn only by trial and error what his group considers acceptable and unacceptable behavior. The greatest insight of the discoveries of childhood may be in their recognition of the need for adults to guide their children into human culture with love, confidence, and understanding rather than by inflicting anxiety, harshness, and punishment. To induce excessive shame and guilt in a child for following innate instincts (or random behavior) divides a personality against itself. The unavoidable self-alienations inherent in the human condition are widened, and so much greater is the work of bringing forth a whole personality in maturity. In a very real way the law does create sin, as St. Paul knew. A sense of guilt may be unavoidable, but to increase the problems of being human by severe castigation creates more harm.

Especially grotesque is the thought of parental rejection and shaming of children for the sake of cleanliness control. If his bodily functions and excretions create loathing and disgust in the significant people who care for him, how can the child avoid feeling that his body is a source of shame. Aesthetic delight in cleanliness must be separated from moral shame over dirt and excretion, both of which are as neutral in nature as rain. All of the New Testament references to dirt and ritual cleanliness invoke Christ's insistence that nothing that goes in or out of the body defiles it; defilement comes only with evil words and actions expressing an evil heart. Some cultures seem to have learned this wisdom better than others. It would be interesting to correlate standards and motivations for cleanliness and acceptance of the body and sexuality. When cow dung is valued for building huts, there is probably little revulsion over the "animality" of coitus, childbirth, or nursing.

A child does well in an environment in which cleanliness enhances order and order contributes to stability, in which these values are subordinate to human relationships rather than the other way round. Antiseptic attacks on germs and fear of disease have to be balanced with acceptance and appreciation of all created things. A child can then feel that his body is neither just a source of danger nor a sacred vessel easily broken. And physical give-and-take in play is as important to a child as the freedom to get dirty while encountering the world around him. Only if well prepared in early childhood for life in general can a small person make better use of explicit instructions and teachings about sexuality.

Without a basic physical self-acceptance and experience of sensuous mutuality and interaction with the world, no sex education can succeed.

Almost all Christian thinking on explicit sexual education has stressed the need to emphasize the mystery and sanctity of sex. Making this an exclusive emphasis, however, seems the wrong approach, if we want sexuality integrated into the personality and into human life. Sex is important, yes, but no more sacred and mysterious than other important things in life. Adults are so suspiciously choosy in their sacred mysteries. Whispered awe, over-seriousness, and the ponderous style appropriate to the cult of a mystery religion do not prepare a child for the realities of sexuality. It is almost impossible for the parent to remain emotionally neutral and detached in instruction, but (and no matter how much technical language he has retreated to) it is far preferable that parents break out in happy laughter rather than subside into silent anxiety. To fearfully suppress mention of the pleasure, play, fun, joy, and delight inherent in married sexuality is to lie through omission. The child can already see for himself, at least to some degree, the struggle, work, difficulty, and adjustments necessary in family life. If the part of his parents' life together that he cannot see is also all grim mystery, then why grow up? Peter Pan has the best of it.

Furthermore, since the child *will* grow up, his first experience in the most innocent form of puppy love will prove all the world's songs, movies, poems, and T.V. commercials substantiated. What, then, will he think of his parent's version of drudging sexuality? Unprepared adolescents are the ones more likely to be overwhelmed by emotions they did not suspect or which they think completely unique to themselves or their own generation. God preserves us and keeps us alive and growing through pleasure and joy, and much of our joy is in sexual delight. Should we not let our children know that they, too, can anticipate pleasure and joy in sexuality. After all, we do not deny the grim side of life in fear of inculcating despair.

In all efforts at sex education, maintaining continual open communication between children and parents is most essential. Things come up again and again in the growing-up process; ideas are assimilated slowly as maturity increases. We all hear only what we can, when we can; selective inattention affects us all. Girls should be encouraged in their sexual curiosity as much as boys. If Freud's theory that girls do not achieve intellectually because they repress curiosity in *all* areas along with "unfeminine" sexual interest, then parents should overcompensate in encouraging interest and supplying information to girls. At any rate, one big conversation (however open and honest), one book, one course in school, will not be enough. All of these must be combined with the opportunities that daily life turns up over the years to add bits and pieces to the child's developing overview.

An inherent idea in the training of children to live in the human community must be the acceptance of the existence of the rights and needs of others. As part of the overall training, the child must learn that he cannot hurt others, cannot destroy their property or steal it, cannot be cruel or bear false witness. The limits of his pleasure, desire, and will begin when other people's rights are infringed upon. This basic respect for others, who also come from God and have their dignity and destiny beyond the moment, should inform all relationships and naturally includes sexual relationships. When sexuality is not exempted and isolated into its own sacred category, then the realization that sexual encounters are personal relationships can come naturally. Our neighbor does not cease to be our neighbor when sex becomes involved. The sensitivity to others and to their welfare and dignity that is inherent in Christian humanist morality will also guide sexual behavior. There is no special sexual morality. Problems come when a sexual code has been isolated from the rest of the morality of human relationships. Parents who lie, exploit others, or compromise their moral responsibilities in other ways cannot teach a sexual morality of integrity, concern, and commitment.

Therefore, while superficial methods and materials for sexual instruction may change, the personal example of the parents (or parent-substitutes) remains central. Books, records, movies, courses, or any other form of conveying sexual instruction will fail if there are no human examples around of people who use this knowledge and practice these techniques to express themselves and their love and commitment to one another. As in other realms, the medium is very much the message. Even parental mistakes and misinformation may not much harm children if the parents' own marital relationship flourishes and if they encourage their children to grow up generally. The best possible method of preparing children for their entry into the world is for the parents to perfect their own human relationships. To keep marriage growing in every direction and dimension involves an effort to completely appropriate one's own body and perfect its orientations to the other, while increasing psychic unity, openness, and self-giving. A strong and happy marriage of loving parents who include play and passion in their love for each other is the best school of sexuality. With a happy family, the necessary balance is built-in. Observing a happy pregnancy, nursing, and development of a much younger sibling is an added dividend. One of the unfortunate results of our cultural pattern of having a few children close together in an isolated family life is the lack of participation in the life-cycle. Children can grow up having rarely seen a pregnant woman, a nursing baby, or an older ill person who dies. Parents have to realize that from birth on they and their children are immersed within a culture which may seriously handicap their efforts.

Unfortunately, isolation, technology, and specialization are all aspects of our modern culture that can become most de-humanizing by destroying empathy and affect. Emptiness and lack of feeling may be our worst symptoms as a society. Thus, the clutching at the straws of sexual emotion should not be scorned. Computers can never know sexual desire. Desire, pleasure, and drive toward other humans help make human beings different from superb supercomputers. The most adequate theories of the self and society seek a synthesis of emotion and reason rather than opting for one or the other. Obviously, only a successful synthesis of emotion and reason makes the successful human being and the successful human culture. It is the goal to which we struggle individually and socially. Sexually, we want and seek desire, pleasure, play, ecstasy, and procreative drive along with self-control, deferment, purpose, commitment, sacrifice, and sublimation. No wonder the cultural pendulum swings from one extreme to another, confusing children, parents, and authorities.

The so-called sexual revolution, however, seems mainly an effort to right the cultural balance and protest against rationalistic impersonality. To restore touch, tenderness, physical community, visions, and dreams to human life can only evoke Christian sympathy. If Christianity had been more whole and true to itself, it would not have become so identified with repression, inhibition, competition, aggression, and authoritarianism. Imagine, for instance, the impact today of a St. Francis on, let us say, the students of California? Stripping himself of all his bourgeois father's clothes in the public square, espousing poverty, communal life, and folk songs, rebuilding churches, going on a peace mission to the enemies of Christendom—would Francis not appeal?

Only a Christianity which has kept its heart as well as its head has the right to preach against excesses of emotionalism or to champion rationality and transcendence. Without heart and spirit, the Christian call to repression for the sake of the community, to discipline for the sake of work and self-identity, to inhibition for the sake of constancy, continuity, and responsibility, sounds hollow indeed. If discipline and denial are not seen as means to more abundant life, if they are seen only as efficient ways to win the "rat race," then why bother? No fasts or stigmata, thank you, unless they accompany brotherhood and an ability to sing canticles of praise to Brother Sun. Only those who love the body and this world and who understand pleasure for pleasure's sake can preach a resurrection worth the listening.

From today's underground youth culture searching for love, community, and vision through drugs, a message comes through loud and clear: Show that Christianity knows that bodies and emotions exist. Even a casual observer can notice a distinct pattern in the depletions in mainstream Christian history. Speaking in tongues and prophesying depart along with instantaneous healing of the sick. Miracles and visions disappear, and saints no longer suffer disconcerting levitations or the phenomena of sweet-smelling corpses. Slowly, the senses, the emotions, and the body have been denied to the point where modern Christians can be embarrassed at the primitiveness of even desiring, much less believing in, personal bodily resurrection.

High levels of self-repression are informally agreed upon, and to drop below the high standards of controlled conformity impairs respectability. The basic necessary inhibitions, sublimations, and repressions have been embellished, extended, and increased to intolerable proportions. The lady of yesteryear who was trained to sit rigidly upright without ever touching the back of her chair lacked the same material support in sexual, emotional, and religious living. Of course, the present social rebel who lies prone on bare mattress or floor expresses a completely opposite view of life. Perhaps our inclining contour chairs are a fairly appropriate cultural compromise. And if contour rockers or swivel chairs be needed to help achieve the delights of the infant's perpetual rocking and rolling motions, so be it. Modern life can well use some soothing motions; those who have not "dropped out" are all too often participating in a kind of continuing "track meet." The complete person should be able to master the disciplines of abstinence, fasting, silence, and contemplation (T. S. Eliot's "teach us to sit still"), as well as to be able to loll or dance about on the floor, shore, or grass. For general usage and cultural ideal, neither a Simeon Stylites nor an Isadora Duncan will do. The complete persons we need to cope with today's realities might be described as ascetic, active, rational, contemplative sensualists. Those speculating on conditions in the year 2000 are worrying over the increasing complexity of life and the fact that "the human mind has a limited capacity for acquiring and storing information."[17] True; but perhaps we should be worrying even more about expanding human emotional and personality development.

Christians must unite with others to struggle for the fullest personal synthesis of body-mind and emotions in the individual and the group. From conception, childbirth, and childhood to death, efforts can be made to preserve and develop the humanness of persons, despite prevailing forces of apathy, disintegration, and disassociation. Again and again we must try to teach our children and ourselves that all rational control, all technology from computers to contraceptives, can be gifts to man and can be used in human ways for human ends.

The Christian affirmation asserts that creation is good, though distorted; and man's work, power, and emotions are good, though also capable of distortion. In human sexuality, as in all human potential, we take the given, develop what we can in love of God and man, and offer our efforts and growing back to God and our human community. As Christians, and especially as Christian parents, we can only hope that our children will join us in this painful and joyful process. Ultimately, the future will be their challenge.

NOTES

[1] Paul Goodman, "Two Issues in Planning," *Commentary,* August 1967, Vol. 44, No. 2, p. 76.

[2] Bernard Häring, *Marriage in the Modern World,* Newman, Westminster, 1965, p. 319.

[3] Cf. Lee Rainwater, *And the Poor Get Children,* Quadrangle Books, Chicago, 1960.

[4] Cf. Charles F. Westoff, Robert G. Potter, Jr., and Philip C. Sagi, *The Third Child,* Princeton University Press, Princeton, N. J., 1963.

[5] Cf. Richard Fagley, "Doctrines and Attitudes of Major Religions in Regard to Fertility," *Proceedings of World Population Conference, 1965,* United Nations, New York, 1967, p. 83.

[6] Cf. A. Y. Boyarsky, "A Contribution to the Problem of the World Population in the Year 2000," *Proceedings of the World Population Conference, 1965,* United Nations, New York, 1967.

[7] P. B. Medawar, "Science and the Sanctity of Life," *Encounter,* December 1966, p. 97.

[8] Alva Myrdal, "Goals for a Population Policy," in *The Family and the Sexual Revolution,* ed. by Edwin M. Schur, Indiana University Press, Bloomington, Ind., 1964, p. 405.

[9] Cf. Anne C. Biezanek, *All Things New,* Harper, New York, 1964.

[10] Erik Erikson, *Young Man Luther,* Norton, New York, 1958, p. 108.

[11] A. S. Neill, *Summerhill: A Radical Approach to Child Rearing,* Hart, New York, 1960, p. 217.

[12] Cf. Helen S. Wessel, *Natural Childbirth and the Christian Family,* Harper, New York, 1963.

[13] Erik Erikson, *Childhood and Society,* 2nd ed., Norton, New York, 1963, pp. 293, 421.

[14] Karl Rahner, S.J., *Theological Investigations,* Vol. IV, Helicon, Baltimore, 1967, p. 152.

[15] Quoted in Hilda Graef, *Mary: A History of Doctrine and Devotion,* Vol. I, Sheed & Ward, New York, 1963, p. 35.

[16] Philippe Ariès, *Centuries of Childhood,* Vintage Books, New York, 1965, p. 35.

[17] George Miller, "Some Psychological Perspectives on the Year 2000," *Daedalus,* Summer 1967, p. 886.